THE LABYRINTH OF DANGEROUS HOURS:
A MEMOIR OF THE SECOND WORLD WAR

Lilka Trzcinska-Croydon

The Labyrinth of Dangerous Hours
A Memoir of the Second World War

UNIVERSITY OF TORONTO PRESS
Toronto Buffalo London

© University of Toronto Press Incorporated 2004
Toronto Buffalo London
Printed in Canada

ISBN 0-8020-3958-8

∞

Printed on acid-free paper

Library and Archives Canada Cataloguing in Publication

Trzcinska-Croydon, Lilka
    Labyrinth of dangerous hours : a memoir of the Second World War /
    Lilka Trzcinska-Croydon.

ISBN 0-8020-3958-8

1. Trzcinska-Croydon, Lilka.   2. Auschwitz (Concentration camp).
3. World War, 1939–1945 – Personal narratives, Polish.   4. World War,
1939–1945 – Underground movements – Poland.   5. Prisoners of war –
Poland – Biography.   I. Title.

D805.5.A96T79 2004   940.54'7243'0943862   C2004-902862-6

University of Toronto Press acknowledges the financial assistance to its
publishing program of the Canada Council for the Arts and the Ontario
Arts Council.

University of Toronto Press acknowledges the financial support for its
publishing activities of the Government of Canada through the Book
Publishing Industry Development Program (BPIDP).

I dedicate this book to my children, Monika and Janek, my daughter-in-law Ellen, my grandchildren: Melanie, Tobias, Evan, and Amelia, and to my brother, Tytus, and his children and grandchildren. As well, I dedicate it to Marina's daughter, Magda, and her family, and to Zosia's children, Jennifer and Gregory, and their families.

I also wish to dedicate my book to the memory of my parents, my aunt Lucia, and my sisters, Marina and Zosia. As well, I dedicate it to the memory of Jerzy Masiukiewicz, Andrzej Makolski, Josef Pleszczynski, Tadeusz Zawadzki, Alek Dawidowski, and to all those young Polish men and women who gave their lives in that cruel war so that Poland could go on being.

Contents

Illustrations follow page 46

Foreword

This account of suffering and survival in wartime Poland is much
more than a simple memoir. It is an exquisite piece of creative writing –
concise, restrained, observant of detail, and ultra-sensitive to emotion.
The author, Helena Trzcinska – now Lilka Croydon – was a lovelorn
teenager when she was arrested by the Gestapo. She was the daughter
of a Catholic family in Warsaw who were engaged in the underground
Resistance and who were all imprisoned with her. When she was
finally liberated at the end of the war by a British soldier with battle-
blackened face, who handed her an egg and a small can of preserve,
she was little more than a breathing skeleton. In the meantime, she had
passed along the fearsome Nazi conveyor belt, which took her from
the Pawiak prison to Auschwitz-Birkenau, to Ravensbruck, and to
Bergen-Belsen.

Lilka's experiences and recollections do not take the form of a
chronological tale. Instead, they are presented in the context of the
moments when they were most intensely remembered, thereby gaining greatly in impact. Hence the exploits of her friends and family in
the Resistance are recounted as she later awaits her fate in a cell in the
Pawiak. The happy hours of a pre-war Christmas Eve are recalled from
the depths of Auschwitz, where Christmas could not be celebrated.
And the unknown fate of the lost boyfriend, to whom she remains
unwaveringly devoted, is not mentioned until the very last pages,
when she is recovering with the Polish army in sunny Italy. After she
and her boyfriend had been arrested in Warsaw, Lilka saw him only
briefly for a few seconds in Auschwitz, where he defied the rules to
whisper 'I love you' in words that were clearly destined to outlive him.
At every stage, there is a poem, to cement a feeling or to capture a
scene in beautiful, brief, and dignified lines:

How lucky
to die so many deaths
and to stay alive.

Lilka's language is marvellously exact and stimulating. For example, she describes her impressions of the death march from Auschwitz to Breslau as 'both vivid and vague.' The emotions of the ordeal were painfully vivid. The names and the appearance of the villages and districts through which the faltering prisoners trudged were necessarily reduced to a blur.

The prism of gender gives the text an important colouring. From the moment that the men were separated from the women at the gates of the Pawiak, Lilka was left in almost exclusively female company. Her fellow prisoners were women. The great majority of their immediate guards were women. And their concerns were often the special anxieties and preoccupations of women. Their predicament only served to highlight the constant anguish of separation from fathers, husbands, sons, and lovers, who sometimes were only on the other side of the wire, but who might well have been on another planet.

Some of the features of this story will be familiar. Most readers will already have encountered descriptions of concentration camp conditions: the gratuitous brutality of club-wielding *Kapos*, the indignities of communal washing and delousing, the Auschwitz tattoos – Lilka was No. 44787 – the hunger and disease, the daily contest with one's mortality. But other things, such as the intervals of normality at work in the camp *Bauburo* or snatches of a BBC news bulletin overheard on a forbidden radio, may be surprising. The Polish aspect of the war is far less known than it deserves. So, too, is the multinational character of the Nazi camps. The picture painted is one of women and girls of all ages and of all nationalities – Poles, Jews, Czechs, Greeks, Germans, Hungarians, and Ukrainians – thrown together, sometimes quite literally, in a squalid, degraded mass shorn of all decency. Yet decency, too, survived in patches, amidst the depravity.

Sixty years on, the generation that lived through the Second World War is reaching its natural term. The survivors and the bearers of memory are, of necessity, advancing in years. In the nature of things, there cannot be many more books of this genre. And there will be none that are more worth reading.

NORMAN DAVIES
Supernumerary Fellow of Wolfson College, Oxford;
Fellow of the British Academy and Professor Emeritus
of the University of London

Acknowledgments

I wish to thank the following persons who encouraged and supported me in writing and publishing this memoir:

Kristina Sieciechowicz, Len Husband, Norman Davies, Johnathan Parry, Antoni Grabowski, Antonia Medwecki, Eva Bartoszewicz, Tamara Trojanowska, Eva Thompson, Irena and Joanna Masiukiewicz-Groszkowska, Wojtek Makolski, Danuta Bytnar-Dziekanska, Joanna Makolska-Kowalska, Anna Lempicki, Jacek and Grazyna Junosza-Kisielewski, Bogdan and Elzbieta Kaminski, Elliot Markson, and Don Carveth.

Guide to Pronunciation

sz is equivalent to *sh*:	Orsza is pronounced Orsha
j is equivalent to *y*:	Janek is pronounced Yanek
w is equivalent to *v*:	Wojtek is pronounced Voyteck
rz is equivalent to *zh*:	Jerzy is pronounced Yezhy
sia is equivalent to *shia*:	Zosia is pronounced Zoshia
cia is equivalent to *chia*:	Lucia is pronounced Luchia
u is equivalent to *oo*:	Ursula is pronounced Oorshoola
drz is equivalent to *dzh*:	Andrzej is pronounced Andzhey
trz is equivalent to *ch*:	Trzcinska is pronounced Chchinska

Camp Vocabulary

Arbeit Macht Frei	work sets you free
Aufseherin	a woman overseer
Bauburo	building office
Blokälteste	the chief of the block
Kapo	the head of a work group
Kommando	a work group
Lager	camp
Lagerälteste	camp director
Lagerstrasse	camp road
Links	left
Posten	a guard
Raus	out
Schnell	fast
Sonderkommando	work group at the crematoria
Stubendienst	helper to the *Blokälteste*
Zugang	a newcomer

Introduction

My Family of Origin

My parents were married on 31 January 1920 in Minsk. The marriage took place during the early years of the newly formed Polish Republic.

At the end of the First World War, in 1918, Poland regained its independence, and much of its former territory, after over 120 years of nonexistence on the maps of Europe due to the three partitions that took place in the eighteenth century between Russia, Prussia, and Austria.

During the years 1918 to 1921 six wars were fought concurrently in Poland. Worst of all was the Soviet war, which threatened the Republic's existence. Polish legions fought under the leadership of Marshal Josef Pilsudski. The Soviet army retreated. The Armistice was signed on 12 October and took effect on 18 October 1920.

My mother's fiancé at the time – the younger brother of Wladyslaw Tatarowski, who was her brother-in-law – was killed in this war. My father participated in this war as a sapper, in the rank of lieutenant.

When my father met my mother, Felicja Masiukiewicz, she was in mourning for the death of her fiancé. My father courted her most ardently until she consented to become his wife.

After their marriage my parents soon moved to Brzesc (Brest) where my father opened an architectural planning and building office. Their first son, Adam, was born in 1921. Unfortunately, he died in infancy. My brother Tytus was born next, on 4 January 1922. My sister Marina followed on 23 August 1923. I was born on 9 July 1925.

Those years in Brzesc, judging from Mother's stories, were happy, even though in economic terms they must have been very stressful, as was life for many in the newly independent Poland. But my parents were young, and they enjoyed a pleasant life in Brzesc with many social events within their circle of friends.

My mother's older sister Lucia also lived with us. She was blind since age fourteen, but in spite of her handicap she was very helpful around the house and was a sort of nanny to us.

In 1928 we moved to Lublin, where my youngest sister, Zosia, was born on 19 November 1928. But the stay in Lublin was not long, and soon we moved to Milosna, a commuter town near Warsaw. It must have been in the year 1929. While we lived in Milosna my father was establishing his office in Warsaw.

My Father

My father, Antoni Trzcinski, was born in Warsaw, around the year 1900, the youngest boy in a family of four sons and one daughter. His father's poor health led to his mother's taking over his tailoring business.

Father became a building engineer, and he also specialized in architectural planning. His career was interrupted by the Soviet war, in which he was an active participant.

His family hoped that, after the war, he'd marry the daughter of a rich Warsaw storekeeper, but instead he married my mother, who enchanted him with her personality and her passionate nature. His family was cold and critical towards this warm and generous woman, who created a household reflecting many of the eastern Polish traditions.

My Mother

My mother's Masiukiewicz family were descendants of the Tatars. Over the centuries Tatars of the Crimea made annual incursions into Poland, but they were also recruited by the country's military rulers as auxiliaries for action against other Christian princes when occasion demanded. Many settled down in Poland. They received from the Polish kings some land and a minor nobility. Many gave up their Muslim faith and married Polish women. Their families became part of the rich Polish ethnic mosaic. The Masiukiewicz family settled in Wlodawa.

Grandfather Masiukiewicz was born in 1847. At the age of sixteen, in 1863, he joined the insurgents of the January Uprising against the Russians. Later, he married a Wlodawa girl, Anna, and together they had ten children. I believe some of them died in infancy and in early child-hood. My mother, Felicja, was the second youngest girl, and Uncle Lucjan was the youngest boy. There was also Aunt Lucia and Aunt Josephine, the oldest of the female siblings.

Grandfather Masiukiewicz worked as a smith, and his oldest son, Jan, joined him in this occupation. Grandmother Anna Masiukiewicz died of cancer in the summer of 1925. Aunt Josephine married Wladys-law Tatarowski, also of Tatar origins, and Mother was engaged to his younger brother, who died in the Soviet war. Mother, after a period of mourning, met my future father in Minsk, and that's where they got married.

When my grandfather Masiukiewicz became very ill in his later years, my parents brought him to a hospital in Warsaw, where he died in 1936. I recall his military funeral in Warsaw, at which a few remain-ing veterans of the January Uprising were present.

My Family at the Time of Our Arrest

From 1929 until 1932 we lived in Milosna, the commuter town near Warsaw. We lived in a large villa with a veranda. The villa was located by a wide road. On the other side of the road there was a beautiful meadow, which was covered in the summer by many varieties of wild flowers. The house had a large backyard, with a pond, some fruit trees, and an outhouse hidden by bushes. There was no electricity or running water in Milosna.

My mother's older sister, my blind aunt Lucia, lived with us, and our grandmother Trzcinska would stay with us, from time to time, for periods of several weeks or months, and then she'd move on to stay with her other sons' families. There was also a maid, Wladzia, to help with carrying water from the well and wood from the shed to the kitchen and to assist Mother with shopping and cooking.

Father commuted, by train, to Warsaw, where he was gradually establishing his office.

We moved to Warsaw in 1932. Our first apartment, with three bed-rooms, was on Elektoralna Street. Marina and I went to a little private school run by the Sisters of Charity, and Tytus went to a local public school. Zosia was still too young to start school. That apartment was rather small considering that there was also a new maid, Stasia, and my aunt Lucia was also living with us.

In 1938 we moved to a larger four-bedroom apartment, centrally located, at 74 Marszalkowska Street. At this point my grandmother used to live with us, and there were nine in our household.

The apartment was on the third floor. It was spacious and bright, and there was a balcony in Marina's and my bedroom overlooking busy Marszalkowska Street. From the balcony you could see the Church of the Redeemer, with its two tall spires. It was my last home in Poland. The apartment building was totally destroyed during the 1944 Warsaw Uprising.

Part I

Fighting Poland (September 1939–May 1943)

1

Dies Irae

Today my voice is choked and mute my flute
My world has disappeared in an evil dream.
Therefore with tears I ask thee:
Those who have poisoned thine air
And extinguished thine light,
hast thou forgiven them?
Hast thou loved them?

'A Question,' Rabindranath Tagore

26 March 1943

To My Sister, Marina

That night, sucked into the city's darkness,
I slept soundly
Neither the distant wail of the murderers' marching song,
nor phantoms carrying moon shadows
through lightless streets
entered my sleep,
while you, vigilant, restless
on your wide bed
thought of our friend's
tortured but liberated body.

Around eleven
you called me awake.
Heavy footsteps on the stairs.

The concierge, voice full of tears,
asked Father to open the door.
Jack boots,
Nazi uniforms,
machine guns.
Vultures' heads
shouting orders:
'Raus! Raus! Schnell! Schnell!'

Why so many armed men?
No one here owns guns.
My little Grandmother has only prayers.
And my blind Aunt?
Her sole arsenal is love.
My Father?
In these harsh war years
he works hard to keep us from starvation.
His wife – a Niobe frightened for her children.
The Nazis came to arrest them
and their three daughters?
Asked about their son?

Hurriedly we dressed.
I stuffed a pink cotton nightgown into a bag.
It might be useful.

As we left I saw,
in the dark recesses of the dining room,
Aunt Lucia's blind despair.
From my little Grandmother's lips
prayers flew towards us.
The maid's loud weeping followed us down the stairs.
Black hearses – three Mercedes limos
waited below.
I sat next to you, grateful for your body
between me and the Nazi.

We drove.
Voices pretending casual indifference,

we talked about the dark, empty streets
to camouflage our hearts' wild beating.
A cupola of darkness
surrounded our wounded city.

At the Gestapo headquarters
we were interrogated, one by one.
Without hesitation,
we repeated our holy lies
as we'd rehearsed
at the dinner table hours before.
We repeated our sacred lies
to protect those in deadly danger,
while over little Zosia's head
the Nazi murderer
shook his whip.
We three daughters
watched as Mother was removed.

We listened:
In the adjoining room
Father, breathing heavily,
with choking voice repeated
holy denials, holy lies
to the sound of blows,
his voice weaker and weaker,
his breathing louder and louder.

Downstairs,
a narrow corridor,
small cells.
Like streetcars:
two rows of narrow seats
filling each.
These cells contained
memories of torture,
these walls had heard
muffled cries from swollen lips.
As night dragged on

I heard Father's snoring,
a sweet lullaby of safety.

At dawn, called out of the cell,
I was given a broom
to sweep the narrow corridor.
I saw the night's cruel harvest.
In one cell, a friend,
his father's head bleeding.
I rushed to my bag
and tore my pink nightgown into bandages.
No one stopped me.
As the sun came up,
we were transported
to the political prison – Pawiak.

We were transported, at dawn, from the Gestapo headquarters to the prison in a crowded truck. Mother was staying close to my little sister, Zosia. Marina and I were sticking together. Did we talk to one another? Most likely not, as our talk would have to be purely banal – we could not say what we really thought or how we felt because the other prisoners were strangers to us. In a way we were relieved to know that we would not be executed – at least not yet – otherwise why would they bother taking us to somewhere else? They could have shot us there and then. I was aware of one heavy reality: that with each moment we were being removed from our life as we knew it, and that from now on some ineffable destiny would run our lives to some unpredictable end. A profound sense of dread was entering my heart, my mind – descending like a heavy mist, penetrating every pore of my skin, wrapping me in a dark blanket of fear and of hatred towards those who had violently taken over my country, my city, my home, and my family.

Finally we came to our destination – the Pawiak prison, a grim building, until then familiar to me because so many of my friends stayed here for longer or shorter periods of time. Usually it was a temporary stopover before they were executed or transported to Auschwitz or Buchenwald. That was the fate of Jacek Tabecki, a young student, eighteen years old, arrested for tearing down a German propaganda poster. He was the first casualty in our close group of friends. He was sent to Auschwitz, where he fell ill with typhus. They wouldn't let him recover from his illness – he was taken to the gas chamber. That happened early on, in 1940. Jacek acted on his own initiative. It was before the Girl Guides and Boy Scouts in Warsaw became part of the Army of the Resistance, called the Home Army, or in Polish, 'Armia Krajowa,' the AK.

After Jacek's arrest we all mourned his departure, and when the news of his death reached his mother, we decided to stop dancing at the modest social gatherings that we held to celebrate our name-days – the feast days of the saints for whom we were named. My boyfriend, Jerzy Masiukiewicz, who was arrested in November 1942, also spent some days in Pawiak, after his interrogation at the Gestapo headquarters. But he was alive in Auschwitz – he was writing letters to his family.

Pawiak prison was located in that part of Warsaw where the Germans created the Jewish Ghetto in 1940, soon after they occupied the city in October 1939. The Ghetto held about half a million Polish Jewish citizens.

As we entered the prison, the women were separated from the men. We were led to a dim office room lit by a desk lamp. A man in a uniform sat behind the desk. He took our names, birth dates, and addresses and confiscated our purses. Then we were taken to a quarantine cell. It was a small room, maybe forty square metres. Against the wall some mattresses were stacked up. High up was a small window with iron bars. In this room we encountered other prisoners who were brought before us. It was a motley group of women, of different ages. Their faces and their attires showed the almost four years of German occupation: tired, sunken cheeks, clothes from before the war times, carefully preserved; women tired of daily line-ups for the basics: bread, potatoes, milk. An elderly woman was showing us terrible bruises on her body, inflicted on her during interrogation. I was wondering how badly my father's body was bruised – was he still in a lot of pain? His snoring during the night in the cell, at Gestapo headquarters, had given me a sense of security about his condition. When I was given a broom to sweep the corridor I noticed that he was in the cell next to mine. To my surprise he was asleep on the floor, his winter coat, lined with beaver fur, spread beneath him. Mother always claimed that he had nerves of steel – last night he proved her right.

The four of us huddled together, creating an island of familiarity amid the unfamiliar and threatening surroundings. My sisters and I were the youngest members of this group: Zosia was fourteen, I seventeen, and Marina nineteen. We talked hardly to anyone, especially if they were asking too many questions. Distrust crept into our minds, and we were afraid of traps. We were surrounded by strangers, and we were determined to keep our experiences to ourselves. This behaviour was instinctive rather than planned. There was an atmosphere of restlessness in this crowded cell as we waited for the next move by our captors.

After some time a woman opened the door of the cell and called out my name. She was wearing a dress that looked somewhat like a nurse's uniform, and she led me from the cell towards the hospital part of the prison. I was mystified and a bit scared as I followed her. We entered what looked like a shower room, and another woman appeared. She might have been in her late twenties – brown hair, a pleasant smiling face, and a friendly demeanour. She introduced herself as Wanda Wilczanska and said that she wished to talk to me.

We were left alone in the sterile, bare room that had, along the wall, a number of shower cubicles with white plastic curtains. She said she had greetings for me from Sawa. It was the pseudonym of our Girl Guide company leader. On hearing her name, I relaxed and lost my suspicious attitude.

Wanda proceeded to tell me, to my great surprise, that she was married to one of my cousins, Witold Bienkowski. I didn't know him personally, but later I found out that he was very involved in an underground movement, Zegota, which was devoted to hiding Polish Jewish citizens and saving them from destruction.

Wanda Wilczanska continued her story. She worked with this cousin of mine in their Resistance group. The Gestapo came to arrest them, but he was out. They arrested her. After she was incarcerated they realized that they were in love with each other. So they got married by proxy, she in the prison, he outside, in the city. All of this sounded terribly romantic and tragic. I looked at her with curiosity and awe.

After this introduction Wanda proceeded to ask me about our interrogation at the Gestapo headquarters. I told her what transpired there during last night, although I had a feeling that those outside already knew. The man who had handed me the broom to sweep the corridor and allowed me check out who was in the other cells, and who didn't protest when I went to fetch my nightgown – to tear it into bandages to dress my friend's father's wounds – that man must have been one of our people.

After our talk, I was escorted back to the quarantine cell. I dared not utter a word about my encounter until we were allocated to our cells. Then I hoped that I would find some privacy to talk to my mother and my sisters about our new relative, Wanda, and about our conversation.

But, unfortunately, we were split up. Mother and Zosia were put together, but Marina and I were separated and put in cells with strangers. When I could find some privacy during the washroom call, I told Mother and my sisters about our new relative, and about our secret talk.

The cell to which I was allocated was fairly large. The windows were quite low, and I could see the prison yard below. Wooden cots with straw-stuffed mattresses were lined up against the walls. The washbasin and the bucket were separated by a curtain, so there was a semblance of privacy in this communal room. There were even some benches and a couple of small tables.

While resting at night on my bed, I went back, in my mind, over the events of the last few days. Until then there had been no time for reflection, and yet so much had happened to me and my family. Going over the events of the night at the Gestapo headquarters I was again overwhelmed by the perversity of our captors. In a way I was grateful that they had removed my mother before they so cruelly interrogated my father. They must have sensed her passionate nature – they got a glimpse of it when, during the initial interrogation, the Nazi said to her: 'Did you know that your son is a bandit?' She would have jumped at the man there and then, had it not been for my father, who held onto her and restrained her in her rage.

How to describe the feelings that I had experienced when my sisters and I were left in a room with a door, purposefully left ajar, to the room where they interrogated my father? We stood there, frozen, not daring to look at each other, as if we were afraid to see in each other's eyes a reflection of our own feelings. That would have made us more vulnerable and less strong to survive this cruel ordeal.

My parents. Does this arrest mark the end of their life together? Twenty-three years of life filled with strife, hard work, love, and sorrow. When they married, Poland had been independent for just a couple of years, after 120 years of non-existence as a free state, wiped off the map of Europe, divided by the three powers: Russia, Prussia, and Austria. After regaining its independence in 1918, Poland still had to continue the war against the Soviet troops that would not leave its eastern territories. Marshal Josef Pilsudski and his brave legions continued fighting the

Soviet troops. Father fought in this war, as well as did Mother's then fiancé. He was killed, in a cherry orchard, by a Soviet bullet.

After this loss, Mother decided to become a nun. However, her confessor was very much against this decision. He claimed that she had no right to close herself off from the world while she had her elderly parents to take care of. At that time, Mother met my future father, fresh from the Soviet war. He was a Warsaw man, born and bred in that city. He was enchanted with her and with all that she represented. She epitomized for him the rich traditions of eastern Poland as well as the romantic and emotional heritage of her Polish-Tatar origins: her passionate dark eyes, her raven-black hair, and her voice full of mysterious intonations that sang the melodies of Polish, Russian, Ukrainian, and Belorussian songs. He courted her with great determination and with full awareness of the recent loss of her beloved: she kept his letters, tied with a red ribbon, letters that Father promised to put in her coffin should she die before him. By the time I saw those letters, they looked old – the hand of time had imprinted a yellow hue on them. Maybe from her stories about her lost beloved I learned that 'love, like eternity, is one.' But that first love never interfered with Mother's devotion to Father. How lovingly she used to talk about their wedding, which took place on 31 January 1920.

A sleigh carries them
through wintry fields to Minsk cathedral.
Distant sounds of Soviet cannons
tremble in January air,
a bouquet of white frozen lilies
trembles on her lap.
A beam of sunlight
lights up their faces.
Her eyes, black Tatar moons
immerse in the Vistula blue of his gaze.
Their last quarrel resolved
over the pot of cabbage rolls
and now they wait
at the side pew.
The cathedral brightly lit up,
red carpet all the way to the altar.
They walk forward, a royal couple.
He wears his Polish Army uniform,

She, a matching suit.
United for struggle and a few happy moments,
frozen white lilies thawing on her arm.
In the bright glow of candles
five tiny spirits
float above their heads,
five tiny ghosts
of their future offspring –
the only family present at their wedding.

In my cell, apart from other prisoners, there was a young Jewish girl about my age. Her name was Mary. She was about my height, with dark, wavy hair surrounding her pale face. I found out from another prisoner, Krystyna Wigura, that Mary had been arrested because she belonged to a Communist Resistance group, on top of being Jewish – a double crime against the Third Reich. My short stay with Mary, in the same cell, made an indelible impression on me, as it was inevitable that the Gestapo would not let her live. Because of our closeness in age, I must have identified strongly with her certain fate.

One day an SS-man came into our cell and told Mary to go with him. She turned to reach for her coat, but he stopped her. She was to go as she was. This usually meant that the prisoner would be executed.

First Death

Before the war,
on behalf of an emaciated horse,
my mother used to
severely reprimand
his indifferent driver.

Mary, a girl my age,
seventeen, maybe eighteen.
We share this prison cell
and our youth.

She moves swiftly,
quietly, fearfully.
Says little,
she is an animal

sensing imminent danger.
At night she chews
an extra bit of bread
she earned sweeping corridors.

Today
they are taking her away.
Mary's dark eyes
look at me with helplessness.
Her despair squats next to fear
in my own, wide open eyes.
My first death – first bead
on a long necklace.
Tear at his swastika-stained uniform
Don't let him take Mary away!

I don't hurl myself
at her captor.
I don't tear, scratch, bite or kick.
I watch, with fear in my eyes.
I watch, heavy stone of silence in my heart.

You are going as you are, Mary,
to your last – my first – death.

After the fall of Communism, during one of my visits to Poland, I
met two of my cell companions from those days, Krystyna Wigura and
Jadwiga Pruszkowska. They remembered Mary. For them it was also
their first experience of death by murder, when one felt totally helpless. They remembered us, my mother and sisters, too. After the war
Krystyna wrote a book called *A Long Lesson*, and the four of us keep
appearing and reappearing in her memories of Auschwitz.

One morning, a couple of weeks after our arrest, I was looking through
the cell window at the prison yard, when to my great surprise I saw
my brother Tytus carrying the garbage out in the yard. I told my
mother and my sisters that he too was here. We had had no idea about
his whereabouts since the night when he came home to tell us that the
rescue party had been successful and that Janek Bytnar was safe, surrounded by his friends and looked after by a physician.

After the war we found out that the plan had been for Tytus to spend the night at the Plucinskis' apartment, located in our building, a couple of floors above. Stenia and Henryk Plucinski were our parents' close friends, and they had known us since we were very young. Tytus went there, but when the Gestapo arrived to arrest us, those people became scared and turned Tytus out in the middle of the night, in the middle of the curfew. The Plucinskis were a childless couple, and they didn't have the guts to stand their ground, even though they were in no danger. It was a cruel act as Tytus could have been shot on the street simply for being there after the curfew.

But maybe I'm too harsh in judging them. How could they know that we wouldn't give away his hiding place during the interrogation? How could they know my father's great strength, that even when severely beaten he wouldn't betray anyone?

Tytus managed to run, in the night shadow of the buildings, to the street where Jerzy Masiukiewicz's parents lived, and they put him up – they were very close friends of ours and distant relatives, on my mother's side. A couple of weeks later Tytus was at another secret meeting, and he was arrested, together with the rest of the participants. He said that he was really lucky that day, for when he walked into the apartment and realized what was going on, he dropped his briefcase, which was filled with guns, behind the open door, and the SS-men didn't notice it. After the war Tytus told me that the meeting he came to attend was in an apartment quite familiar to him because he used to deliver packets of the weekly *Information Bulletin*, the paper printed by the underground press for distribution to members of the Home Army, to that location.

During our brief exchanges, at washroom breaks, I talked to my mother and my sisters about the fate of our blind aunt Lucia and our eighty-year-old grandmother. My worries about Aunt Lucia overshadowed my other concerns. I wondered whether, in reaction to our arrest, she again developed her dreadful allergy, as it always flared up when she worried too much about some family problem. Her face would swell and turn dark pink, and her blind eyes would sink deeper into their sockets as she gazed helplessly around. These symptoms were accompanied by high fever. Who would take care of her? Grandmother would, most likely, pray more ardently than ever. Of course, Aunt Lucia would join her in her prayers. They always competed with each other over who would praise God more devoutly – maybe this time they would forget about this competition and join each other in their prayers. But how would they manage when the rent money ran out, when the food ran out? When one of them became ill? Mother hoped that other relatives would take care of them. After all, Grandmother used to visit, over extended periods of time, her other four sons' families. True, she didn't get along with her other daughters-in-law as well as with my mother, but now she had no choice. But what about my beloved Aunt Lucia? Who would take care of her?

Aunt Lucia,
her name meant light – a cruel joke:
at fourteen light left her eyes.
Her seeing fingers rolled out the dough
for plump pierogies, ribbons of macaroni.
A white apron wrapped her long black skirt,
grey hair covered by a kerchief,
flushed face smudged with flour.

To her belonged the ritual of our weekly bath.
A large wooden tub set in the middle of the kitchen.
On the wood stove bubbled large kettles of water
while we, taking turns in this homemade sauna,
squealed and splashed,
her gentle hands soaping, scrubbing small backs,
scrawny necks, pink shells of ears.
In her tobacco-smelling embrace
I spent hours listening to ghost stories.

We went for walks,
here a stone, there a puddle,
my five-year-old eyes watched the path
for both of us,
tripping only over Hail Marys
or Ten Commandments,
as for the love of my Aunt,
for my first communion
I memorized heavy words,
cardinal and mortal sins,
and attempted to separate
wishes from deeds,

magic from reality,
and felt the first torments of conscience.

Aunt Lucia,
more loved than my little grandmother,
who for hours mended
the family's worn-out socks and other garments,
glasses sliding
to the tip of her pointed nose,
lips whispering prayers.
In shape and bearing –
a Mrs Tiggywinkle.
Later,
'pigeon blood' was her condemnation
of our polished fingernails,
teenagers' shy attempts at sophistication.

My reverie about those two members of the family was again over-shadowed by concerns about our own fate. However, one overwhelming emotion in the midst of this uncertain life was the feeling of happiness that the rescue party had liberated our friend, Janek Bytnar. He was free, surrounded by his family and friends. These thoughts were also foremost on Marina's mind as Janek was her beloved. Janek Bytnar (pseudonym Rudy) was a close friend of Jerzy Masiukiewicz (Maly), Alek Dawidowski (Dlugi), Jacek Tabecki (Czubek), and Tadeusz Zawadzki (Zoska). All attended the Batory Gimnazjum, and all were members of the Twenty-third Scout Company and, during the occupation, of the battalion 'Zoska.' As for me, having last November suffered anxiety and anguish after Jerzy's arrest and deportation to Auschwitz, I could feel for Marina and identify with her pain and her relief at knowing that Janek was safe after his terrible ordeal of interrogation. Besides, Janek was also a dear friend of mine. Whenever he and Marina had had a disruption in their relationship, he'd ask me to go for walks with him, and then he would unburden his sorrows and his fears to me. I was proud and happy in this helpful function, but Jerzy was not too happy about these walks. So I had to spend a lot of time assuring him that Janek's love for Marina was the main theme of our talks.

One glorious Sunday in autumn our group had set out for a picnic in the Kampinos Forest. This beautiful forest was located on the outskirts of Warsaw suburbs and could be reached by car or by a streetcar – after getting off at the last stop one still had to hike, for about an hour, to reach the woods. Jerzy was not able to come due to some other commitment. Nor was Marina with us. Maybe it was due to a temporary break-up with Janek. But Janek, Wladek Slodkowski, Irena Masiukiewicz, and Danuta Bytnar were there. Janek and I spent most of the time together. He unburdened his aching heart to me while we walked over purple, heather-covered meadows, surrounded by the intensely beautiful autumn colours of maple trees with their red hues, slim birches dressed in yellow, and huge oak trees with their amber and yellow leaves. The happy chirping of finches and sparrows formed a stark contrast with Janek's expressions of pain and sorrow. His large, blue eyes were full of sadness, his expressive face framed by his ginger-blond crop of hair. My compassion was profound, and I was beginning to think that Marina should be told about the enormity of pain that she was causing. When I reached home that evening, I talked to Marina and asked her to be kinder to Janek. She became very annoyed with me and told me to mind my own business. I guess she was right. From then on I didn't interfere with her relationship to Janek. I should have remembered that as soon as spring came they would be happily together again. It seemed to be a pattern of their relationship.

Love and war. Maybe love triumphs more passionately in times of death and destruction than in times of peace and security. Eros, the god of love and life, must assert himself more powerfully at times when Thanatos threatens around every corner of daily life. That's what was happening in my country.

I'm trying to remember what the worst aspects of my incarceration were. Undeniably the loss of freedom was one – the constant uncertainty about tomorrow was another. Worry about the other members of my family – young Zosia, Mother, and Father.

Mother – always concerned about others. Her vivid imagination would fill her with frightening scenarios. She must have worried constantly about the fate of Tytus before she learned that he was also in the prison, with us. Before our arrest Mother used to beg Tytus to let her carry clandestine papers or guns and deliver them to the other members of the Resistance. Her reasoning was that no one would suspect a housewife of carrying these forbidden objects. At least she had Zosia in the cell with her, and they could comfort one another.

And what about Father? How was he dealing with his imprisonment? His gentle and seemingly unemotional nature might have helped him to accept this tragedy with equanimity and calm. But underneath it all there was a deeply feeling man, used to resolving family problems, used to being responsible for our fate and our well-being. He had never objected to clandestine meetings at our apartment – even though he must have appreciated more than anyone else the dangerous consequences. It was his way of supporting the Resistance movement, of supporting our active involvement in defiance towards the invader. This incarceration must have taken away from him his fatherly position as protector – he was now unable to take care of us.

I was so glad that Zosia was with Mother – they needed each other. I wished that I could have shared my cell with Marina. I missed her company. How was she doing? Her worry about Janek must have been enormous. In the quarantine cell her beautiful chestnut-brown, wavy hair framed a pale and worried face. We'd shared a bedroom for the last few years, and now we were apart, unable to share our thoughts, our hopes, our sorrows.

Other aspects of life that made things difficult were the total lack of privacy, the line-ups at prescribed times for the washrooms, the lack of exercise and the inactivity, combined with life so uncertain and so devoid of purpose – except the purpose of survival.

I also wondered about my friends in the city. What had happened to the other rescuers? How was Janek? In my cell I was surrounded by older women, and I missed the company of more contemporary companions. I knew from Wanda that my friends outside were informed of our arrest.

I had been planning to meet with Joanna Berland on Saturday, 27 March, to go with her to an emergency clinic in the Praga district, on the other side of the Vistula River, for our practice, which was part of our secret training as military nurses. With this training we would be able to serve as first-aid nurses in case of an uprising against the invader. Of course, Joanna wouldn't expect me to be at the clinic.

Joanna Berland was my closest friend. We had both attended the same high school since 1938, and as she lived just around the corner from me, we walked together to classes. She lived with her parents. Her two older half-sisters were from her parents' previous marriages, and both were now married. Joanna grew up among adults, without the company of contemporary siblings. Therefore, my home was very appealing to her – we always had something going on, with young people constantly coming to visit. Before the war her parents took her to France and Italy, and I loved listening to her stories about those trips. Once she told me that she had always admired my femininity, which was in contrast to her rather boyish style of clothing – she usually wore rather short, pleated skirts, woollen knee-highs, and sports shoes. Her wavy, blond hair was cut short, and she didn't seem to be too concerned about its style.

When the war started, Joanna moved from her apartment to another part of the city. I thought it was for economic reasons, as her father was a lawyer and his practice would be non-existent during the occupation. But soon I learned the real reason. One day I was talking to Joanna and another friend, Marysia Wysowska, and at one point in the conversation Marysia said to Joanna: 'You do have such a Jewish way of looking at things.' I had no idea what she was talking about, and I said so. To this Joanna explained to me that she was Jewish but was trying to keep it secret. She had moved with her parents to an obscure part of town, where they lived under an assumed name. In this way they wouldn't have to go to the Jewish Ghetto. The reason for my ignorance was simple: Joanna didn't 'look' Jewish, her name sounded German, as many Polish names did, and she was of the Evangelical faith. Whenever at school we had our religious instruction from a Catholic priest, she would leave for her Evangelical instruction. I guess that my parents knew that Berland was a Jewish name, but they never mentioned it to me. She was my closest friend, and this is what mattered. I wondered how Joanna was – I was sure she would be devastated by the news of our arrest.

In my cell, some of the women talked about the circumstances of their arrests and even enjoyed revealing their secrets, but I kept my story to myself, not wishing to endanger anyone. I spent long hours playing solitaire, chatting, reading, and in games of bridge with my companions. I was very proud of this new accomplishment. I'd learned to play bridge just a few months before our arrest. I played with Joanna Berland, Wanda Jedraszko, and Marysia Wysowska. We felt so sophisticated. As there was, at that stage, an early curfew hour, we decided one day to stay in Joanna's apartment and play late into the night. Her parents agreed to this folly. After all, Joanna spent many nights at my home if we had a lot of homework and wished to work on it together. We would joke, saying that this game of bridge would come in handy if any of us were to be arrested. And so there I was, in prison, killing time by playing bridge.

Some of the women who came from the outside to work in the prison had smuggled in a few books. We read those in no time. And, of course, there was my capacity to daydream. I had no idea what a blessing it would prove under these difficult circumstances. In normal life it sometimes became a handicap.

It nearly made me fail my first year of high school, in 1938. My love for Jerzy was still not being reciprocated – he was first enamoured of my beautiful sister Marina – but during classes I couldn't stop thinking of him and daydreaming of being with him. I loved his tall, slightly stooping body, his large, blue eyes and dark eyebrows, his gentle smile. I hoped that one day a miracle would happen and he'd look at me with the same admiration as he looked at Marina. When Mother went for the spring-term interview with my teachers, she was sorely disappointed with me and gave me a severe talking to. As such discipline was quite foreign to me – I usually only too eagerly complied with all my parents' expectations – I was shaken and remorseful and promised to get myself out of the mess as quickly as possible. I worked very hard, and by the end of the year all my 2s (Ds) became 3s (Cs), and I passed.

2
Gone with the Wind

Our vacations in the summers of 1938 and 1939 were spent with our distant cousins, the Masiukiewicz family. The friendship between our families was fairly recent – only since 1937. By then we'd lived for several years in Warsaw, after moving there from the commuter town of Milosna.

We came upon these cousins thanks to my blind aunt Lucia, who'd lived with us ever since I could remember. In the winter of 1937 she had to go to the hospital for some treatment. One of the nurses attending to my aunt, on hearing her name, Masiukiewicz, asked if she was related to the doctor Michal Masiukiewicz who worked at the hospital. As there existed, in all Poland, only one Masiukiewicz family with Tatar roots, my aunt replied that yes, she was related to that doctor, even though they had never met.

After some time Mother contacted Michal Masiukiewicz and invited him and his family to dinner. It turned out that Mother and our newly found relative hàd a common great-grandfather who had had two sons – one was Mother's grandfather, the other one was his.

When we heard that there were two teenagers close to us in age in this newly discovered family, we were very eager to meet them too. It turned out that Jerzy was of the same age as Tytus, seventeen; Irena was fourteen, and therefore in age between Marina, who was fifteen, and me, thirteen. My younger sister, Zosia, was ten at the time.

My mother and Ania Masiukiewicz soon became very close friends, and in the following months we met many times at each other's homes to celebrate our name-days and other holidays.

In 1938 Tytus and Jerzy were attending their last year of high school. Irena and Marina were also in high school. For me 1938 was a memorable year as it was my last year of elementary school and I was to start high school by September. To be accepted to a state school we had to pass a very tough examination – those who failed ended in private schools, with lower standards. In June 1938 I passed this exam and was admitted to Julius Slowacki Gimnazjum.

Mother and Aunt Ania started to plan a summer vacation for us. They decided that it would be lovely to spend the summer at the ancient town of Kazimierz, located by the banks of the Vistula River. The town had existed since the fourteenth century, since the reign of King Kazimir the Great. Tytus and Jerzy went for the month of July to their Boy Scout camps, and would join us in Kazimierz in August. Our fathers were staying in Warsaw but would visit on some weekends.

The villa that our mothers rented was lovely and spacious, surrounded by shrubs of mock-orange and lilac. It was a short walk to the sandy beach and the ravines that surrounded the town. On each end of the town there was a hill. On each hill there were ruins of a royal castle. One castle used to belong to King Kazimir the Great and his royal family; the other castle was built by the king for his mistress, the beautiful Esther. That story lent a romantic flavour to this place, and I often thought about the king, riding at dawn on his white charger through the sleeping town after a night spent with his beloved.

As Norman Davies writes in *God's Playground: A History of Poland*:

Kazimir (1310–1370), the only Polish ruler to be deemed 'Great,' was known for his skills of diplomacy and statesmanship. Almost every aspect of Polish life was carefully scrutinized and reformed by him. He was instrumental in codyfying and publishing the whole corpus of existing Polish Law – it became the base of Polish Law for the next four centuries. Poland, unlike most countries in Europe, escaped the scourge of Black Death. The arrival of numerous Jewish refugees from Germany marked a further stage in establishing the greatest concentration of Jewry in Europe.*

In the little town of Kazimierz the square in the centre of town contained many booths and stalls where the Jewish merchants displayed their wares and the peasants from the surrounding villages would

---

*Norman Davies, *God's Playground: A History of Poland* (New York: Columbia University Press, 1982), 95–6.

crowd in to buy whatever they needed. The sight was most lively and typical – the peasants in their colourful country attires and the Jewish men in their dark suits, long beards, and skullcaps. When the war started I often wondered about the fate of those Jews who, in my memories, were so much a vital part of this and many other Polish eastern towns.

I recall that one of the main attractions of this vacation was an event in which Marina and Irena were to take part. One weekend a show was planned by the local organizers for the vacationers. Both Marina and Irena were invited to participate, with a group of other girls, in the show. Their part was to dance a minuet. Every day, for a week prior to the performance, they went to the rehearsals while our mothers made beautiful white tulle dresses for them. Finally, the day of the performance arrived and many guests gathered around the small meadow surrounded by the ancient ruins of the royal castle. Jerzy, Tytus, and I watched our sisters gracefully dancing to the tunes of Paderewski's minuet, played by the local band.

Every day we went to the local beach for a swim in the river, and later we wandered in the nearby ravines and meadows. With every day Jerzy's admiration for Marina grew, while my brother was increasingly impressed with Irena's beauty. This vacation strengthened the bonds of friendship between our families, and the year that followed was full of social gatherings and holiday celebrations. My loving feelings towards Jerzy were growing with each visit, even though the reality didn't encourage any hope that he'd reciprocate these feelings.

The summer of 1939 was again spent with our cousins. Our mothers rented another splendid villa, on the banks of the River Bug, near the little town of Rybienko, in eastern Poland. Tytus and Jerzy again spent the month of July at their Boy Scout camps, but they joined us for the month of August.

One day some visitors arrived from Warsaw for Jerzy. They were his friends from the Batory Gimnazjum and members of the same Boy Scout company. One of them was Janek Bytnar, and – to my great joy – it was love at first sight for him and Marina. I felt truly sorry for Jerzy, who must have experienced remorse, jealousy, and pain. Janek was a slim fellow, not as tall as Jerzy, with a mop of blond hair and a broad smile. Another friend who accompanied him was Alek Dawidowski, a very tall and handsome young man, also from the same class at school.

There was also Jacek Tabecki, a long-time friend of Irena and Jerzy – he was very much smitten with Irena, and I believe that she reciprocated his affection. I think that my brother, Tytus, was also in love with Irena, as she was a very beautiful girl. All the boys had just received their high school diplomas and were looking forward to their university studies in autumn.

We spent happy days going for walks along the River Bug and sometimes, late in the day, joining the shepherds, sitting down with them to bake potatoes on the bonfire and sing country love songs. One song particularly comes to mind about a shepherd boy waiting by the well for his shepherd girl. He wonders why she doesn't come to his well for water. Is she afraid or only shy? She replies that if she were afraid of him, or shy, she'd throw herself into the well. They both come to the conclusion that they love each other, and they end by stating that it is easier to fall in love than to fall out of it. As we sang this simple love song, our hearts were with the words, and each of us identified with those two by the well.

After several days our visitors departed for Warsaw, and the five of us roamed the countryside, swam in the Bug, and experienced the powerful pangs of first love.

We were shaken out of our pleasant existence, one summer evening, by a tremendous explosion. Next morning we went to Rybienko to see if we could find out what had happened. The town was in turmoil. The bridge on the River Bug had been blown up.

Like most towns in eastern Poland, Rybienko had a multi-ethnic population, and the Jewish community was very large. That day, by the synagogue, there gathered groups of Hasidic Jews, in their black coats and their black hats, in agitated discussion. We couldn't find out who was responsible for the explosion. The word 'war' was on everyone's lips. But if it was the anticipated war with the Germans, then why was this bridge blown up? It was located in the eastern territories. Surely, it would take a lot of time for the German armies to get there. Little did we know that the Soviets were also planning to invade Poland and that the Bug would become the border between the two invaders. That August the Germans and the Soviets had signed an agreement of neutrality. The 'Molotov-Ribbentrop' pact also included a secret protocol that divided spheres of influence and enabled the Soviets to expand into eastern Europe. It must have been the Soviets who had blown up the bridge.

Soon Father arrived from Warsaw to help Mother bring us home. We caught the last train to Warsaw. On 1 September 1939 Hitler attacked Poland – the war with Germany was on.

As the train was taking us home, the enemy planes showered the railway tracks with bombs. Fortunately, they missed our train, and as soon as we got to Warsaw we were led to an air-raid shelter where we waited for the all-clear. Aunt Ania and Father and Mother, with their young broods, miraculously managed to catch taxis home.

Marina and I found that Father had turned our bedroom into a pantry, with sacks of flour, potatoes, sugar, dry beans, and rice. Huge hams and strips of bacon were laid out on the shelves to help us through the war. Mother was very impressed by Father's far-sighted planning.

On 3 September 1939 our radio brought encouraging news: England had declared war on Germany and a few hours later France had followed. The relief was enormous – we were not alone.

I've just described the beginning of the war against Poland. We were at the threshold of days, weeks, and months of continuous terror, constantly tightening its iron grip on the whole nation. At that time ignorance of what was to come was a blessing.

3
Resistance

When we returned from our summer vacation Warsaw was under
siege. Schools were closed. Daily bombings forced us into the basement shelter where my sisters and I indulged in reading countless novels. In breaks between the howling of sirens announcing an air raid
and the gentler 'all-clear' sirens, we'd run to the local library to
exchange our books. For once in our school-age years the reading of
novels wasn't looked down on as an escape, and we celebrated this
change to the full. Aunt Lucia was delighted as I was able to read to
her for unlimited lengths of time. *Gone with the Wind*, in Polish translation, came out just before the war started, and it was one of many novels I read to her. Sometimes when Jerzy was not too busy he would join
me in reading to her – we would take turns, while his arm embraced
me lovingly. In my poem 'A Tangled Garden' I describe those unforgettable days:

> Don't worry
> the war will be over in a week
> while I read to you in our basement shelter
> a funny story about two who stole the moon.
> Mother said I shouldn't laugh.
> The war is on.
>
> This war lasts too long.
> Bombs fall from the sky
> like bad dreams from the ceiling.
> The cellar isn't safe,
> It's scary upstairs.

Days tumble around me
nights in fiery brightness
challenge the daylight.
For once I'm glad you're blind.
Your heart would break
at the sight of this burning church
Its flaming spires – two stumps.

The siege is over.
Our city – a burnt-out crater.
Und der wilde Knabe brach
Roslein auf den Heiden
I sing to you a sad song of a rose.
Come with me.
I shall read to you of war in Atlanta
while Marina takes down
yellow curtains in Father's study
for a new dress.
Every beautiful girl in Warsaw – a Scarlett O'Hara.
Every tender one – a Melanie.

You are God's cruel joke
my beloved one:
He named you Lucia
but took your light away.
Your small, dark world
is becoming too small for me.
I move away in countless ways.
No more imaginary devils
for real ones march through the streets of my city.
Their dress – invaders' uniform.

Dark years, take me.
Lead me in
and out of months full of passion,
nights streaked with terror,
days filled with hope.

As soon as the wailing of the sirens started we would bid our cat
goodbye and go down to the basement of the building. There we

would spend the night or part of the day, sitting on the floor, together with other tenants. Zosia told me that one night Marina, before falling asleep, remembered that she hadn't fed our cat before coming down to the basement. As Zosia was also awake the two of them ran up to the third floor and entered our apartment. The sight through the windows was incredible. The sky was full of fire and smoke from exploding bombs, which were falling all around. They found the food for the cat, and they checked the alcove in which Aunt Lucia and Grandmother should be asleep, for both refused to come down to the cellar. They saw Aunt Lucia sitting on her bed, reciting the Rosary. Grandmother was nowhere to be seen. They ran to Marina's and my bedroom. Grandmother was kneeling on the floor of the balcony, her thin, white hair, which was normally tied into a bun, flowing in the wind, her arms stretched out to heaven, in the direction of the Church of the Redeemer whose two spires were burning. Her lips were repeating prayers, and tears were flowing down her face. They left her there, sensing that she needed to complete that tragic ritual and express her pity and sorrow to her God.

This procedure of going down to the basement was soon declared unsafe. Many apartment buildings were being bombed, and the people hiding in the basements would be buried alive under the rubble, with many suffocating before it could be removed. It was recommended instead that a family should choose one room in the apartment, with only one or two external walls, to accommodate the entire household for the night. In our apartment such a space was our dining room. We removed the dining-room table and chairs as well as the large side-board to Father's study, and we covered the floor with all six of our mattresses and bedding. Grandmother and Aunt Lucia remained in their safe alcove, which had no external walls, and the maid continued to sleep in the kitchen, which also had only one outside wall.

Once, in this communal dormitory, Mother woke up in the middle of the night calling out to all of us: 'They're coming, they're coming!' We were torn out of our restless sleep and sat up, one after another, rubbing our eyes, straining our ears to hear the hateful rumble. The faint glow of the moon lit up the room and our tense faces. After a while we could also hear a faint noise. But this sound was coming from our cat, curled up safely by Mother's pillow. 'Oh, Mama, it's the cat purring, not the airplanes.'

One evening the air raid was very heavy. Many buildings were burning all around us. I had heard that, as the incendiary bombs often fell on the roofs, it was possible to dismantle them before they blew up. Feeling very self-righteous I went out of our apartment to face the crowd of mainly male refugees sitting in the staircase. I made an impassioned speech beseeching them to take turns on the top landing, watching for those bombs that fell on the flat roof of the building. My fourteen-year-old heart fell when nobody moved in response to my speech. Then I wondered if I had asked for too much.

I remember clearly our relief, mixed with horror, when at the end of September 1939 the sirens stopped wailing, the planes stopped flying over our city, and the bombs stopped falling. From the newly arrived refugees we learned that the German armies were approaching our city. Our Polish army, poorly equipped with cavalry horses against the German tanks, was yielding to the superior strength of the enemy. Now we waited with trepidation for the invasion of our city.

One day a woman acquaintance, Mrs Borodzicz, came to call on Mother. She was excited, almost hysterical, when she proceeded to tell Mother what she had seen. She described, with great enthusiasm, a unit of the German army marching through our Marszalkowska Street. How orderly and well equipped they were, how impressive in their tall boots and army hats! Mother listened for a while, but then she couldn't contain her rage any longer. She told the woman to stop praising the enemy. Didn't she feel anger and resentment towards those who had been killing the citizens of this city for one whole month, murdering civilians, children? Ruthlessly destroying the city with their continuous shelling and bombing? Anger and resentment were in my mother's voice, and I felt proud of her.

On Thursday, 28 September 1939, at 1:15 p.m. on the grounds of the Skoda factory in Rakow, General Tadeusz Kutrzeba, after twenty days of heroic defence of the city, signed an act putting an end to the defensive action.

Next day, in the morning, the Polish delegation appeared at the headquarters of the German Eighth Army under the command of General Blaskowitz – where the ceasefire was established from twelve noon. The final signing of capitulation was put off until the next day as the Germans wished the mayor of the city, Stefan Starzynski, to be present.

On Friday, 29 September, the Warsaw Garrison gave up its arms and prepared to leave the city.

On Sunday, 1 October, the units of the Tenth German Division, which were part of the German Eighth Army, marched into Warsaw.

Hitler, during a meeting on 2 October 1939 with H. Frank, head of the General Government (the Warsaw–Krakow area), made the following declaration: 'For a Pole there may exist only one master, a German master. Two masters can't exist side by side. Therefore, all the representatives of the Polish intelligentsia must be killed. It sounds cruel, but it is the law of life. The General Government region is a Polish reservoir, a great Polish labour camp.' The same month Germany annexed the rest of Poland.

Hitler's executioners would exterminate the Polish intelligentsia through the following methods: extermination of individuals through execution and destruction in concentration camps; social degradation of this class by depriving members of their professional positions and even moving them to the worker ranks; prevention of further development of this class by closing high schools and universities as well as cancelling all scientific and cultural activities that would enrich the national culture; dissemination of propaganda intended to influence the remaining social classes by blaming the intelligentsia for the mistakes leading to the September defeat.

On the streets of Warsaw there were crowds of people, their faces sad and grave. There was no chaos. The destruction of the city was horrendous. Many buildings had grenade wounds, with roofs broken and partly torn off. Many were split by bombs from roof to basement. These buildings looked especially terrible: they showed the interiors of apartments with traces of recent family life – beds made up for the night, paintings on the walls, curtains and flowers in the windows, books on the shelves, and dishes, furniture, and clothes broken or torn.

The city, on the threshold of occupation, was deprived of water, electricity, and gas, with demolished transportation facilities and centres of commerce, and inactive postal and telephone services. Streets were covered with glass and rubble, and the crosses of thirty-eight temporary cemeteries gave the city a sad and mournful look.

Crowds of Warsaw citizens gathered in places where the Germans were giving out soup and bread. At first there were six such centres, later twelve. Even though the Germans used this action for propaganda purposes, photographing the queues, people were taking advantage of it, knowing that the food came from German plunder of the Polish soil.

At the beginning of the occupation, very few grocery stores were open, there was a great shortage of products, and transportation from outside Warsaw hardly existed. The most difficult challenge was to obtain bread, potatoes, and coal. From 4 a.m. onward, people lined up in front of stores that sold the bread baked in the city. Banks and other financial institutions had kilometre-long line-ups, and they were paying out only fifty zloty at a time.

Just before the German armies had marched into Warsaw, the mayor, because of atrocities committed on men in other occupied cities, had announced on the radio that all men, aged eighteen to fifty, should leave the city. So Father and Tytus, Jerzy and Uncle Michal, Janek and his father, and countless other sons, fathers, and husbands abandoned Warsaw, leaving behind women, children, and elderly men.

My mother, grateful for the supplies that Father had accumulated before our return from Rybienko, where we had spent our last summer holidays in a free Poland, started cooking large kettles of soup for all of us and for the refugees who were sleeping on the staircase in our building.

After a few days, the refugees gradually dispersed, some to the west, some to the east. Our life became one of endless anticipation for Father and Tytus's return.

During these difficult early weeks of occupation Mother became an entrepreneur, and she involved all her women friends. In our severely damaged city, there were great shortages of food. Many coffee houses were bombed out, and those that were still intact couldn't produce baked goods due to the shortage of flour and other important ingredients. Bombing destroyed the railway tracks, and deliveries from the country were slow and unpredictable. Mother knew that her strength lay in knowing how to bake. The sacks of flour were still there, and so were sugar and butter. She could bake, but she couldn't take care of sales and deliveries. Here she needed her friends.

She'd get up at dawn to start her baking. Delicious smells of sweet buns would reach my nostrils every morning and were an incentive for getting up. By the time I would appear in the dining room most of the buns would be gone, but Mother always left enough for us. We delighted in the aromatic taste of these delicacies and admired Mother's capacity and determination. Next morning, the women would bring the money, minus their commission, and would order more buns.

I recall one woman in particular. She appeared one morning and introduced herself as a friend of Mrs Borodzicz – she must have been about sixty. She wore a wide-brimmed black hat and a somewhat old-fashioned long, black coat. She was very sociable, and my mother always offered her coffee and some buns for her breakfast. The lady rewarded us with great tales about her life, and particularly about her wedding and her fantastic trousseau. I could listen forever to her descriptions of the fine porcelain, sparkling silver cutlery, damask tablecloths, and fine linens. And then, after her coffee, she would head off into the real world, where she would try to sell a couple of Mother's buns for some meagre pennies. The next morning her cheerful voice would call out from the entrance vestibule: 'Mrs Trzcinska, Mrs Trzcinska, today I would like to order four sweet buns for my clients!'

In those days we spent many hours taking turns in lining up for water. There were several centres in the city where water was flowing and available if you had a pail and lots of time to wait in line. All this seemed a part of an incredible adventure that was turning all our lives upside-down.

Soon on the city walls huge German posters started to appear with a variety of instructions, orders, and threats to the population. The curfew hour was announced as obligatory, under the threat of arrest. Jewish Poles were to wear a white armband with a blue Star of David.

At the same time Warsaw was gradually emerging from the horrors of the September siege. Windows were being repaired, rubble was being removed from the sidewalks, unsafe remains of bombed-out houses were being dismantled. Bicycle rickshaws, driven by young men, appeared on the streets, enabling the citizens to travel around the city.

In late October, Father appeared in the front hall. Such joy at seeing him. He looked bedraggled, with sunken cheeks and deep shadows under his eyes. After a few days he recovered enough to want to take over Mother's business. 'You use too much butter' – always economical, he would criticize her efforts. And in the evenings he would tell us about his adventures on his voyage east. The main highways were very crowded and dangerous because the German planes would send showers of bombs onto the refugees.

He kept to the lesser roads, staying overnight with villagers. He marvelled at the multitude of dialects in different parts of the country. In general people were kind and helpful to him. By the time he reached the vicinity of the Bug River he realized that he was in just as much danger there as in Warsaw. The Soviets were eager to send to the gulags as many of the Polish intelligentsia as they could find. The news from occupied Warsaw didn't indicate that he would be shot the moment he arrived there. The invaders, he heard, were making themselves at home in the city, and so far there had been no mass executions. So Father decided that his place was with his family.

But where was Tytus? They had split up, and Father had lost track of our brother.

Soon we heard that Uncle Michal and Jerzy were back, as well as Janek Bytnar and his father and most of Jerzy's friends. A stranger appeared one day at our door with a note from Tytus. He had carried it all the way from Kowno, a city in Lithuania. Tytus informed my mother that he was well and waiting for an opportunity to get to Sweden, from where he hoped to go to England to join the Polish army units there.

Mother was completely undone by this. She fantasized about Tytus being in the Royal Air Force, endangered at every moment by the *Luftwaffe* sending showers of bullets at his plane. Or she imagined him serving in the Royal Navy, his submarine blown up in the mid-Atlantic. When she had recovered from her fears, she was determined to travel to Kowno to bring Tytus back. No amount of persuasion could stop her. She borrowed some country woman's clothes from our maid, and with a babushka tied under her chin and some money in her bag, she set out on this perilous journey. Father carried on with her bun-baking business, and we prayed for her and Tytus's safety.

By the end of November she and Tytus returned, safe but exhausted and emaciated. Mother, after crossing a couple of 'green' – meaning illegal – borders, reached Wilno (Vilnius), found a refugee centre, and from there sent a note to Tytus, in Kowno, that she had come to bring him home. While waiting for his answer, she spent hours in a church in Wilno in front of the image of Matka Boska Ostrobramska, the Holy Mother of Ostra Brama, known for its miraculous powers. Soon my brother appeared at the refugee centre where she was staying. What could the poor fellow do? Moved by Mother's determination to have him home, he cancelled all his plans for travelling to England. They returned, after illegal night crossings of more 'green' borders and long hikes between rides from the local peasants.

On St Nicholas's day, 6 December 1939, to celebrate all the returns and all the reunions, my parents threw a party for us in our apartment. Jerzy Masiukiewicz and his sister Irena came, as well as Janek Bytnar and his sister Danuta, Jacek Tabecki, and Wladek Slodkowski, plus the four of us: Tytus, Marina, Zosia, and me. Wladek was the most senior member of our group – he must have been twenty. We'd known him for a number of years. In 1935 my parents had rented a villa, for the summer vacation, in a commuter town, Wesola. It was close enough for father to come from Warsaw on Saturday evening and stay until Sunday night. It was a large villa, with a tennis court. We met a number of young people in the community, and Wladek was one of them. During the day we played tennis, and in the evenings the tennis court became a place for social gatherings and sometimes we danced to the newest tunes. One of them was the American song about the three little pigs and the big bad wolf. Wladek was a nice young man, and as he was quite a bit older than most of our male friends, my mother, whenever we wanted to go to a party in the neighbourhood, always asked if he would be going there as well. In this way he became our chaperon. Our friendship with Wladek continued after we returned to Warsaw.

Tytus, Jerzy, and their friends were now eighteen. Marina was sixteen, I'd turned fourteen the previous summer, and Zosia was ten. Irena and Danuta were also sixteen. Despite what seemed like large differences in age we seemed to ignore them, for we were joined by a common adventure: living in an occupied city, with the hated enemy imposing many restrictions on our lives. One way to deal with this situation was to hold onto a secure circle of friendships that would enrich our lives. During the occupation we didn't go to the movies, which were 'Nur fur Deutsche' – only for the Germans. The same applied to theatres and public concerts. Musical afternoons we would organize, from time to time, privately in our homes.

On 6 December, after a delicious meal consisting of roasted chicken, Russian salad, cold cuts, and tomato-and-cucumber salad, with Mother's walnut torte for dessert, we listened to stories of the boys' wanderings, and of Tytus's adventures in faraway Lithuania. Later we danced to tunes played on an old-fashioned gramophone. Our favourite was the Andalusian Tango. Jerzy wasn't too accomplished at dancing tangos, but he later confessed that he loved dancing because he could hold me close to him.

This gathering gave the start to other social meetings at our home. We were drawn to each other by friendship and, in some cases, by the beginnings of tender, adolescent love. One such meeting in particular comes to mind. It took place sometime in February 1940. As usual, it was a Sunday afternoon. This time I came up with an idea that had been with me for a while. I said that it was wonderful to gather on Sundays for social reasons. But since there was so little to enrich our lives during the occupation – no radio, no cinema, no concerts, no theatre – shouldn't we try to spend our times together working on some interesting projects? Everybody applauded my idea, and we proceeded to plan our cultural activities.

The first meeting took place on 25 February 1940, to establish the rationale for our group's existence, to give it a name, and to appoint an executive. Decisions were to be made by a democratic vote. Many ideas came up regarding the name of this group, but finally we settled on Our Circle of Mutual Admiration. The name reflected the gentle romantic affiliations developing between some members of this group – Marina and Janek, Irena and Jacek, Jerzy and me.

In the following weeks a number of papers were presented. Tytus, because of his great interest in theatre, gave one on The History of Theatre in Poland. Wladek wrote on Attraction, Friendship, and Love. His presentation promoted a lively discussion, for each of us felt ourselves experts on the subject. Among other papers were Culture and Civilization, What Is Music?, My Relationship to God, My Ideal Society, and Socialism and Capitalism.

Our circle gradually dissipated because of other commitments. But even though the formal meetings didn't take place at regular times, we continued to get together for picnics in the Kampinos Forest, for a swim by the banks of the Vistula River, and at parties to celebrate our name-days. During many of these trips a friend of Jerzy, Andrzej Zawadowski, whose hobby was photography, accompanied us and immortalized most of us in black-and-white photographs. Some were taken on the banks of the Vistula, some in the Kampinos Forest.

Thanks to Jerzy's sister, Irena, many of these photographs have been preserved, as she and her mother spent the Warsaw Uprising in Milanowek, a commuter town near Warsaw, avoiding death and preserving these treasures. Uncle Michal worked in the field hospital during the uprising.

My love for Jerzy, finally reciprocated, turned this first spring of the German Occupation into a time of quiet enchantment, of quickened heartbeats, hands hungrily searching hands, shy embraces, furtive glances that said what lips weren't ready to say.

That spring of 1940, my young body unfolding, I was given a pink satin bra, an external sign and confirmation of my budding womanhood. I kept it in a drawer, and once in a while I would put it on – gradually getting used to its unfamiliar grasp.

One day, in my wish to share my secret with Jerzy, I led him to my room and whispered: 'I want to show you something.' I took out of the drawer that pink satin secret, with its two small cups. I let him hold it in his trembling hands. He looked into my eyes, and then slowly, with reverence, he lowered his face towards the two satin petals and tenderly kissed the insides of each cup, lingering and burying his lips, his face, in the future mysteries locked in the pink softness. As I watched this silent ritual I knew that I would always love him.

The schools reopened at the end of 1939. After a few weeks my high school, on Filtrowa Street, was taken over by the Germans, and we had to attend classes in an ugly commercial building, closer to the city centre. This school also received a new name, indicating that the curriculum would no longer be for high school, with a high academic content, but for that of a commercial school – since the Poles, viewed as subhuman by the Germans, did not need higher education. But all this was just in the name. In reality, we continued our studies just as before the war. Mrs Helena Kasperowicz, the principal of our high school, and all her teachers were determined to defy the Germans' new curriculum, even at risk to their own lives. Actually, as time went on, quite a number of them were arrested.

When we were still in our old school building, Jerzy would often pick me up, and we would walk home together, through the Mokotov Field, avoiding the main streets, where the enemy's presence reminded us of the grim reality. Those walks home were the highlight of our day – in the early dusk, in the shade of the trees, we were able to give our feelings some physical outlet through shy, tender kisses and gentle embraces. These delicate and tentative physical manifestations, in my strictly and devoutly Catholic perception, were sinful, and later on, at church, the act of confession ruined their pleasure. I went through terrible moments when I had to describe to the priest not only my innocent deeds but also my not-so-innocent fantasies. So one day I decided to make a clean sweep of all the cobwebs on my conscience, and to cover all the embarrassing details I told the priest that we went 'all the way.' Nothing could have been further from the truth, but I waited, kneeling, for the sky to fall down, or for the earth to open up and swallow me whole, or at least for the priest to send me to some remote and strict convent, where I would spend the rest of my days repenting the sin I didn't even commit.

I was almost disappointed when the priest told me to say, for several days, ten Hail Marys a day. As I was leaving I glanced back, for the priest was leaning slightly out of the confessional, as if he wanted to see what this young Magdalen looked like. All he could see was a fifteen-year-old girl, dressed modestly in a school uniform. If he could see inside my heart, he'd know that I had confessed a big lie to avoid going into details of my gradual and gentle discovery of the best parts of my young life – my budding sexuality, and my tender love.

Jerzy and his friends attended Vavelberg School, supposedly a low-level technical school, but the curriculum was really that of a polytechnic, with university content and high academic standards. This was also another manifestation of the secret defiance of the occupier's orders.

Soon other activities, on top of classes, started to fill up our spare time. Boy Scouts and Girl Guides became an underground organization, named the 'Grey Ranks,' and soon we became part of the Home Army – the Army of the Resistance. There was secret military training for the Boy Scouts, paramedic training for Girl Guides, and involvement for all in the Petty Sabotage.

In the spring of 1942 I had been sworn in as a member of the Army of the Resistance by Sawa, head of our Third Girl Guide Company. Before my arrest I was being trained as a military nurse. A young physician gave secret classes in anatomy at my home to me and several friends from my unit. After the lectures in theory, we took practical training in emergency clinics in Warsaw hospitals. The focus was on first aid as we were preparing for an uprising against the Germans. Soon Joanna Berland, Marysia Wysowska, Wanda Jedraszko, and I formed a Medics Club. We were devoted to our training, and we all planned to become physicians.

When Jerzy and I talked and dreamed about our future together, we saw ourselves as a married couple. He, as a mechanical engineer, would become director of a car-manufacturing plant, and I, as a physician trained in social medicine, would take care of the workers and their families – the plant would be run as a co-operative.

Marina, who was no longer a Girl Guide, was involved in the Resistance by keeping a mailbox for Janek, who was a leader in the Grey Ranks and the man she loved. If anyone had an important message for Janek they would deliver it to Marina, and she'd pass it on to him. In this way his home address could remain secret, known only to those who were his close friends.

Apart from being trained as a paramedic, I participated in some activities of the Petty Sabotage. It was important to let the people of Warsaw know about us and that a fighting Poland existed, even though our fighting, so far, was limited to secret preparations for the uprising, secret school classes, and patriotic slogans chalked on the walls. The slogans changed – sometimes it was a schematic picture of a turtle, signifying sabotage by slow work in factories. Then there was a picture of an anchor – the central, upright part ending with the letter 'P' for Poland and the two bottom parts in the shape of the letter 'W' for *walczaca*. The anchor said, symbolically: Fighting Poland.

I was assigned – just weeks before our arrest in March 1943 – with Marysia Wysowska, a friend in my unit, to cover the walls of the houses on a street in my neighbourhood with anchors – for Fighting Poland. Our assignments had to be carried out just before the curfew hour, when there were few people on the streets. Marysia lived nearby. I went to her house at the appointed hour. But her aunt, who like my aunt Lucia was a sort of nanny in Marysia's family, became suspicious, and when we told her we had to deliver a book to a friend nearby, she insisted on accompanying us. This unexpected twist ruined our plans, and we had to improvise. We dropped off the fictitious book at an address of a fictitious friend, and Marysia had no choice but to return home with her aunt.

I was resolved to carry out my assignment without her. I was very nervous and also furious with Marysia's aunt for ruining our plans. I reached the designated street and proceeded to draw with chalk the anchors in broad strokes on the walls of the buildings. The street was empty, but after a short time I heard footsteps behind me.

I stopped printing and furtively glanced back. There was a man following me. I kept walking towards our apartment building. I was extremely worried, wondering if he had seen what I was doing. As well, I was in a dilemma. If I went home and he followed me, I would get my whole family into trouble. However, if I stayed on the street after curfew, I would get into trouble for sure. To test him, I crossed the street. Sure enough, he crossed as well. But maybe it was just a coincidence, and maybe he lived close to my home. I decided to go home, as I still hoped that his following me was just a coincidence and my nerves were making me read too much into it. So I entered the main entrance to our building and started to climb the stairs. To my despair, he was following me. I started to run, two steps at a time. Then he stopped, and I heard his voice, loud and clear: 'May I have a date?' On hearing this, I burst into stifled, hysterical laughter, mixed with tears, as I climbed the stairs even faster. He stopped his pursuit, and not hearing any answer he must have left, for the curfew was just minutes away.

All was quiet when I reached our apartment. I rang the bell, and my brother opened the door. He was obviously upset and asked me where I had been – didn't I know that it was dangerous to be on the street just before the curfew? Half laughing and half crying, I told him what had happened. Tytus was furious with me and made me promise that I would never do such a foolish thing again. I promised. He was absolutely right. When I reflected on this incident, I concluded that my nervous behaviour, as I was glancing around me, must have appeared to the young man as an invitation to follow me, and he had responded.

4
Rescue

Towards the end of 1942 arrests of members of the Army of the Resistance in Warsaw were increasing. It seemed as if the Gestapo had managed to trace some important connections and was systematically raiding secret meetings and arresting many participants. In Warsaw, we had a sense that the circle of arrests was tightening around us and that arrest was becoming a real possibility for many of us in the Resistance movement.

Early one morning, in November, our front bell rang, followed by an urgent knocking on the door. Marina, in her dressing-gown, opened the door to find, to her great surprise, Janek Bytnar in a greatly agitated state. He came to notify us of Jerzy's arrest, the previous evening, at Urszula Glowacki's home, where he attended a secret meeting. All the other participants were also arrested, including Urszula and her mother.

Jerzy's arrest stunned and overwhelmed me. He was interrogated at Gestapo headquarters and then imprisoned in Pawiak. After a couple of weeks he was deported to Auschwitz.

A grim memory of our conversation, about a year earlier, came to my mind. After we had read in the secret paper *Information Bulletin* about the atrocities committed on prisoners in Auschwitz, Jerzy expressed a wish to go there so that he could see if those stories were true or merely propaganda against the Germans. Ironically, his wish came true.

Long-stockinged, new-breasted Venus
Last night they arrested your young Adonis.
This cruel Minotaur demands daily

hundreds of youths and maidens.
Give me the thread, my dearest Auntie,
your young Ariadne can't find her way
out of this labyrinth of dangerous hours.
Pray for me,
pray for me now
and in the hour of my arrest.

When they finally came in March 1943 to arrest Janek Bytnar and his father, we all knew that the final hour was near. Janek was cruelly tortured during his interrogations, as the Gestapo knew they had one of the key figures of the Grey Ranks, part of the Army of the Resistance, in their hands. He, heroically, didn't betray any of his friends, giving his interrogators only the names of those who were already in the Gestapo's hands. This infuriated them even more, and they vented their anger on his poor, tormented body. After several attempts his friends, including my brother Tytus, finally obtained permission from the top leadership of the Grey Ranks to organize a rescue party – to liberate Janek before it was too late.

The trucks that transported prisoners from Gestapo headquarters to Pawiak always took the same route. The rescue party chose a spot on that route, and there they were waiting, in the ruins of a bombed-out house. In the area of the crossing of Bielanska and Dluga streets waited two units armed with grenades and pistols and one unit equipped with Molotov cocktails; in the nearby ruins were a few machine guns.

In the central position stood a young man, Stanislaw Broniewski, pseudonym Orsza, who led this action. One hand in the pocket of his coat held the loaded pistol. He was watching another young man who was supposed to signal as soon as he saw the approaching truck. Orsza was annoyed, as that man, instead of watching the designated street, averted his head away from it. But suddenly he turned around, and taking off his hat, he started to wave with it.

Orsza immediately put the whistle to his mouth and blew a short signal. Each second now seemed an eternity. Passers-by seemed like an enormous mass with many secret agents among them. Along Bielanska Street there came a motorcycle with the German militia patrol. Fortunately it disappeared around the corner. Here and there appeared German uniforms. But never mind, the action had to go on.

Finally, from around the corner appeared the familiar shape of the prison truck. Palms tightened around the Molotov cocktail bottles, around the cold steel of pistols. At the last moment, a Polish policeman emerged from one of the buildings. He saw, with disbelief, the pistol in the hand of one of the rescuers. 'Get out of here,' shouted Tadeusz Zawadzki. Bewildered, the policeman pulled out his revolver and aimed at Tadeusz, who simultaneously shot at the policeman, who fell down, holding onto his side with one hand while with the other he fired a few shots. In an instant the prison truck, sensing something, turned into the nearest street. Too late. From the sidewalk jumped out several young men, and soon there was the sound of broken glass, and there were flames coming from under the hood of the truck. Instantly, the fire spread to the driver's section. The driver pressed on the accelerator, and the vehicle moved slowly by the Warsaw Arsenal. Two SS-men jumped out of the burning front of the truck. Another SS-man ran from another direction towards the spot where Alek Dawidowski was in charge of the grenades. The SS-man managed to get hold of his pistol and screamed something in German. Alek slowly and steadily took aim and killed him on the spot.

The SS-men who jumped out of the burning truck were shooting chaotically around them. In return, the Polish shots came from the ruins. A sharp salvo of the machine guns joined them. After a few minutes three bodies in German uniforms lay on the pavement. One body was burning. The driver by the steering wheel was also on fire. Only one of the SS-men who had jumped out of the car was using his machine gun. He was shooting steadily and carefully. The crisis was resolved by Tadeusz, who ran straight towards the man. Behind him ran another Polish rescuer. The SS-man was giving up psychologically. He hid behind the truck, but a Polish bullet from one of the running rescuers hit him.

Alek ran to the back of the vehicle and opened up the door. Speechless prisoners threw themselves towards the exit, stepping over the body of a prisoner who was lying on the floor. Only after the miraculously liberated prisoners left the truck did the figure of Janek appear, crawling on all fours towards the exit.

'He's here, he's here,' shouted a joyous voice. Their crazy happiness, together with the excitement of just-finished battle, made the rescuers oblivious to the greenish yellow of Janek's complexion, his sunken cheeks, a huge black bruise under one eye, his grey-blue ears, and his huge, wide-open eyes. They took him in their arms and carried him to the car. He was groaning with pain; the car started. They reloaded their guns and only then smiled at Janek. He looked at them with wide-open eyes. On his face, despite the contractions of pain, appeared a pale smile. He grabbed Tadeusz's hand and held fast to it. His hands were black and swollen. 'Ah, Tadeusz, if you only knew ...'

There were casualties on both sides, and one of Janek's best friends, Alek Dawidowski, was fatally wounded. Five escorting SS guards were killed and three wounded. Twenty-five prisoners were freed.*

My brother had kept us informed about all these plans, and on the evening of the rescue action we were waiting, nervously, at home for his return. Mother was pouring tea, Father lit his pipe. Zosia started to spread her books at the far end of the long dining table. She still had all her homework to do, and as the dining room was the cosiest place in the whole freezing apartment, she was resigned to doing it there, despite all the distractions unavoidable in a space filled with six other members of our family. Most of the distractions came from Marina and me. We were talking about a book that was, apart from *Gone with the Wind*, the most popular one in our circle. The book was there, on the table: *History of England* by André Maurois.

Our eighty-year-old grandmother was sitting across from us. She was the least obtrusive member at this family table, her eyes on a page of her inseparable prayer book, her spectacles at the end of her long nose, her lips moving noiselessly to the rhythm of the prayer. Every now and then the spectacles slid down from her nose and dropped with a faint clatter on the yellowed pages of her book. She would pick them up with her clumsy fingers and adjust them expertly back where they belonged. Her eyes, after this distraction, wandered from face to face, as if looking for disapproval – she was always promising to have her glasses mended. Then she resumed her quiet talk with her God.

Up against the tile stove, outside the bright circle of the light falling from the chandelier above the table, stood my blind aunt Lucia. The tile stove, besides its warmth, so welcome to her rheumatic body, was also in a strategic position, as it was next to the door to the vestibule. From there she would be the first to hear Tytus's familiar steps on the staircase. She was always the first to welcome people at the door. Her joy was in being the first to receive whatever news they brought.

---

*As I'm writing this it is 6 January 2000, and today, in the news program from Poland, I heard that the man who had orchestrated this rescue party, Stanislaw Broniewski – Orsza – died last week, in Warsaw. My description of the rescue action is taken from the Polish version of Aleksander Kaminski's *Stones for the Rampart*, originally published by the underground press in 1943. This version is from the 1956 edition printed in Katowice. Translation from the Polish is my own.

Mother was becoming tense – this time Tytus was later than usual. The grandfather clock in Father's study was ticking away the last minutes before the curfew. 'Why is he so late tonight, why does he do it to me? He knows the horrors that cross my mind during these minutes of waiting,' Mother complained. Father refilled his pipe and gave her a quick glance, tinged with impatience. 'You know he'll be here on time' – but his voice, even if he wished to make it sound casual, had a twinge of annoyance.

We all knew there was reason enough for anxiety. After the events of the last few days no one in the circle of our close friends went to bed at night without wondering if this would be the last night in the comfort of clean bedding and the warm feeling of safety. Janek's arrest and the news of his interrogations were the main reason for this anxiety.

Finally, Tytus arrived just before the curfew, his face flushed, his blue eyes shining feverishly. He was still agitated as he described the events that had taken place just a couple of hours earlier. We were thrilled to find out that all had gone according to the plan and that Janek was in a safe place, being looked after by a physician, surrounded by his friends and family.

My brother's function was to collect all the arms and deliver them to a nearby apartment. He hurried frantically as the curfew hour approached and there was no time to lose. One thing worried Tytus. When they had freed the prisoners one of them had been slightly wounded and kept saying he had nowhere to go. When Tytus looked for him later, after he took care of the guns, the fellow was nowhere to be seen. This person knew all the participants in this action, and Tytus worried that if the Gestapo caught him they would torture him most cruelly to obtain the names. But as Tytus and all who were involved in this action were going to spend the night at different addresses, there was no danger that they would be arrested.

We ate our dinner hurriedly, and I recall Marina refusing to eat the dessert: delicious pancakes filled with sweet cream cheese. She was always so concerned about her weight that even during this time of great shortages she restrained herself and refused desserts.

During dinner it was decided that in case the Gestapo came to arrest us, we all should have the same story to tell. We agreed that the best way was to make my brother a 'good-for-nothing' youth who was only interested in making money on the black market. We, his sisters, didn't want to have anything to do with him or his friends, who had the same interests as he. And, anyway, we hadn't seen him for a while as he went to the eastern territories to do business. We didn't know if the Germans would believe our story, but we would give them no other.

After telling us about the rescue, my brother left to spend the night in the same building, in the apartment of our friends, the Plucinskis. Mother begged Father to go with him, but he refused, saying his place was with his family.

I was invited to spend a weekend in Lukaszowek, a country estate near Warsaw, in the early spring of 1943. It was mid-March and the country-side was still wrapped in snow, although the sun was becoming stronger and a weekend in Lukaszowek looked very promising. I travelled there with Joanna Berland and Wanda Jedraszko, by a streetcar to the end of the line, and there, at the final stop, young Wojtek Makolski was waiting with a horse and buggy.

It was not the first time that I had made this trip. Wojtek Makolski's mother had invited me to spend the last summer at their estate. Her husband and their older son, Jedrek, were hiding, somewhere in Warsaw, from the Gestapo. Actually, Jedrek was staying with Jerzy's family, and that's how I got to know him. We met in the Warsaw Botanical Gardens. Jerzy introduced us, and the purpose of this meeting gradually became clear. Jedrek explained that his mother lived on their estate near Warsaw with his younger brother Wojtek, who was fourteen, and she would appreciate some company over the summer. Apart from the fact that I would bring some life to their isolated existence I could also help in their vegetable gardens, which the gardener usually took care of, but during the harvest time an extra pair of hands would be useful for gathering ripe tomatoes, green beans, and other vegetables for the market. This prospect thrilled me, as during wartime summers we had no chance to get away to the country. After the formalities, which included a meeting of my mother with Mrs Makolska, the plan became a reality.

After several days of my stay in that beautiful place, surrounded by great linden trees, chestnuts, and ash, as well as shrubs of mock-orange with the scent of jasmine, lilac bushes, and beds of resplendent red roses, I learned gradually about the ulterior and real reason for this invitation. The Kampinos Forest hid the secrets of buried guns and munitions from the battles of September 1939, when Poland, over-whelmed by the much stronger armies of the invader, had had to sur-render its independence, but not all its arms.

On weekends, Jerzy, Josef Pleszczynski, and Tadeusz Zawadzki arrived from Warsaw, and with Wojtek they disappeared into the forest, to emerge after some time with mysterious boxes. After their departure, and after Mrs Makolska had gone to sleep and the gardener had disappeared into his house, Wojtek and I would carry one of these heavy boxes into the garden shed. There, by the faint glow of the oil lamp, we oiled the guns and the munitions. The soft light would fall on our young faces while our hands were busy with the cold steel of guns. We were silent during this sacred ritual, and apart from the faint sound our hands made, there was only an occasional hollow sound coming from an owl in a nearby tree. In the air there was a scent of burning oil lamp, mixed with the smell of fear. After a couple of hours we would leave the rest of the work for the next night. We had to finish our task before the following weekend so that Jerzy and his friends could rebury the guns in their little graves, in the forest, where they would wait till the Warsaw Uprising.

It was dawn on Monday, 22 March 1943. I was riding in a buggy, holding the reins, steering the horse, who seemed to know this road better than I did. I was singing a joyous song, one of the waltzes that Miliza Corius sang in the pre-war film *The Great Waltz*, and the young man riding a bicycle along the road accompanied me with his whistling. He was handsome and dashing, with a shy smile and a short moustache, à la Count Josef Poniatowski. His name was also Josef.

After our weekend in Lukaszowek we were returning to Warsaw. The fields around us were still white with snow, and the forest surrounding the fields looked dark and mysterious, even though the previous day we had walked its paths and touched the snow-covered branches. It seemed then that we were alone in the whole quiet world. Josef wanted to kiss me. 'No,' I said – not sternly, but tenderly – no, for we both had our sweethearts in that terrible hell, in Auschwitz, and they needed all our love to hold onto. He seemed to understand, and we walked back among the ancient trees to the house, with its white columns, leaving behind us the dark forest with a heavy snow cloud above and the 'caw, caw' of the black crows.

Inside the salon, the fire in the fireplace was warm and flickering gaily. Shadows moved through the rooms, noiseless feet shuffled gently. I thought, how strange – this house was full of living ghosts of those who had had to abandon it, to hide, to live in fear, adopting strange names, wearing hats and dark glasses so that the enemy wouldn't notice the sadness in their haunted eyes. But they seemed to be here, invisible but present, listening to our conversations, to Chopin's Nocturnes and Preludes played so beautifully by Josef.

Now I was driving the buggy, the horse was trotting 'clip clop,' 'clip clop.' At the back lay three sleeping figures: Wojtek and my two school friends who had joined us for the weekend. We were going to catch the streetcar that would take us to our homes in Warsaw, while Wojtek would ride back to Lukaszowek.

I can still hear the horse trotting, 'clip clop,' 'clip clop.' I can still see Josef's gentle smile, his tender gaze touching my face, my hands, while the 'caw, caw' of the black crows accompanied us on this last trip.

Four days later the Gestapo arrested me and my family. Josef Pleszczynski was killed eight months later, in November 1943, during an armed action called 'Wilanow' against the Nazi occupiers. He died in Jedrek Makolski's arms.

When the Gestapo came to arrest us they were very particular in their search of my brother's room, but as he had expected this visit, he'd cleared up all the incriminating papers.

I was dressing hurriedly, but at the last moment I stuffed my pink cotton nightgown into my large red purse. A sudden thought had occurred to me: what if I get my period in the prison? At least I could tear the nightgown up into pieces and use them as sanitary napkins. Of course, I had no idea that for the next two years my periods would stop and the only blood that would stain my pink nightgown-turned-bandage would be from the head wounds of my friend's father at Gestapo headquarters.

After my brave brother Tytus had left for our friends' apartment that fateful night, we also made sure that there were no incriminating papers or notes in our desks. I never kept any addresses of my friends – I knew them by heart. The only thing that concerned me was the secret drawer in my desk. I kept it locked because it contained my journals, and I didn't wish anyone to read my thoughts and dreams about Jerzy. Would they pry it open?

Father, in the last minute before retiring, had stuck the latest copy of the underground paper, *Information Bulletin*, behind an oil painting in the dining room. When I saw him do it I thought how casual he was in this gesture – this was the most unlikely spot to suspect.

Felicja Masiukiewicz, Lilka's mother, at the age of sixteen, 1912

Zosia, Lilka, Marina, and Tytus, Warsaw, 1931

The three Trzcinska sisters: Lilka, Zosia, and Marina, Warsaw, 1935

Felicja Masiukiewicz-Trzcinska, Tytus Trzcinski, Lucjan Masiukiewicz, Lucia Masiukiewicz, and other participants at the military funeral of Lilka's grandfather, Warsaw, 1936

Jerzy Masiukiewicz, Jacek Tabecki, and Alek Dawidowski, on a skiing trip in 1939

Jerzy's name-day celebration, at his home in Warsaw, 23 April 1942. First row: Ania Masiukiewicz, Antoni Trzcinski, and Felicja Trzcinska. Second row: Irena Masiukiewicz, Marina Trzcinska, Zosia Trzcinska, and Lilka Trzcinska. Top row: Jacek Tabecki, Tytus Trzcinski, Alek Dawidowski, Tadeusz Zawadzki, and Jerzy Masiukiewicz.

Jerzy Masiukiewicz on Krucza Street in Warsaw, 1942

Lilka Trzcinska, 1942

Lilka Trzcinska and Jerzy Masiukiewicz, spring 1942

Marina Trzcinska and Janek 'Rudy' Bytnar, spring 1942

Marina Trzcinska, Irena Masiukiewicz, Joanna Berland, and, above, Lilka Trzcinska, on the banks of the Vistula River, summer 1942

Janek Bytnar, Warsaw, 1942

Jerzy Masiukiewicz

Josef Pleszczynski

Marina Trzcinska, Wladek Slodkowski, Lilka Trzcinska, and Jerzy Masiukiewicz, by the banks of the Vistula River, 1942

Irena Masiukiewicz, Marina Trzcinska, and Joanna Berland, by the banks of the Vistula River, 1942

Jacek Tabecki, Andrzej Zawadowski, and Tytus Trzcinski, Warsaw, 1942

Tytus Trzcinski, Danuta Bytnar, Lilka Trzcinska, Janek Bytnar, Tadeusz Kozlowski, and Marina Trzcinska, on the road to the Kampinos Forest, near Warsaw, 1942

Jedrek Makolski

In foreground: Tadeusz Kozlowski, Wladek Slodkowski, Marina Trzcinska, and Janek Bytnar; in back: Jerzy Masiukiewicz and Lilka Trzcinska

Andrzej Zawadowski, who took all the wartime pictures

Wojtek Makolski, Warsaw, 1946

Lilka Trzcinska in Porto San Giorgio, 1945

General Anders's Girls' School in Porto San Giorgio, 1945. In the centre is Captain Wyslouchowa. Zosia Trzcinska: bottom row, fifth from the left. Lilka Trzcinska: second row, ninth from the left.

View from Lilka's dormitory, Porto San Giorgio, 1945

Lunch in Porto San Giorgio, Easter, 1946. Lilka Trzcinska is in the centre, Zosia Trzcinska on the far right.

Zosia Trzcinska, Porto San Giorgio, 1946

Students from Lilka Trzcinska's class, 1946. Lilka stands, far left.

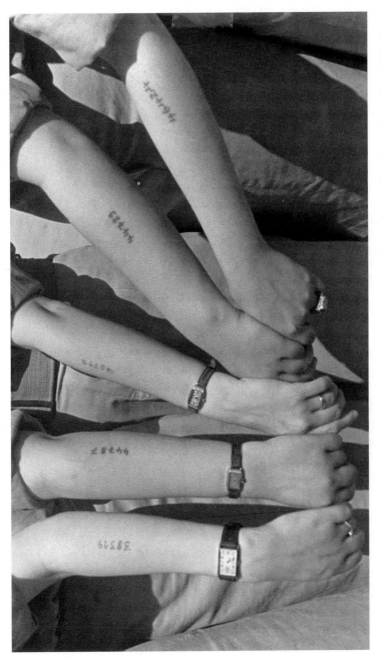

Arms with Auschwitz tattoos: five students from the school in Porto San Giorgio, 1946. Lilka Trzcinska is No. 44787; Zosia Trzcinska, No. 44789.

Lilka Trzcinska, Porto San Giorgio, 1946

Zosia and Lilka Trzcinska, Porto San Giorgio, 1946

Lilka Trzcinska, Porto San Giorgio, 1946

Marina Trzcinska and Alicja 'Ala' Sieciechowicz, in Porto Recanati, Italy, 1946

Tytus Trzcinski, in General Anders's army, Italy, 1946

Zosia Gorska, Porto San Giorgio, 1946

Part II

Auschwitz (May 1943–January 1945)

5
Nos. 44786–9

One day in April 1943 we heard the sound of shots outside Pawiak, in the Ghetto. Our first thought was that our prison was being liberated, but we soon found out that it was the start of the Jewish Uprising. Soon bright explosions illuminated our cell, and gradually we saw some of the houses burning, people running and shouting, shots being fired. Some elderly and religious prisoners started daily prayers for the Jews who were being slaughtered. Soon we all joined in the singing of hymns in solidarity with the heroic, dying Jews. The singing of hymns and prayers resounded in the cells even when the sounds of the uprising moved away to a more distant part of the Ghetto. The uprising started on 19 April. By 16 May, fifty-six thousand Jews had been massacred, the uprising came to an end, and the destruction of the Warsaw Ghetto was complete.

By 12 May we were told to prepare for a transport – one thousand men and one hundred and twenty women prisoners in all. The Germans had organized this large transport partly to remove the prisoners from the area under siege, partly to make room for the new arrivals, as many arrests were taking place because of the increasingly daring activities of the Resistance. As well, on the night of 12 May there was a Soviet air raid on Warsaw. We watched the explosions through the windows, hoping that a bomb would drop on the prison and free us all. It didn't happen.

At dawn on 13 May 1943 we were lined up, in fives, in the prison yard, against the grim, red-brick walls of the prison. Across from us were rows of barefoot men prisoners. We were taken to the railway station by trucks.

I've always loved train trips and have very fond memories of travel-

ling with my mother and my brother and sisters to my Aunt Josephine's estate in eastern Poland. Those summers, when we were still
very young, Mother used to take us away for two months. We loved
the excursions into the ancient forest, where we picked mushrooms
and blueberries, as well as the hay rides and other pleasures of country
life. However, the train trip that we were about to take, to an unknown
destination, was like no other before.

Each train ride – a ride into unknown future,
into recovered past.

Trains of my childhood, nostalgic whistles,
where are you? Where are you black dragons
spouting steam, hissing and snorting?
Inside this iron monster
a cozy cradle of my mother's arms
as we travel from Warsaw, eastward to my aunt's farm.
We arrive at some dingy station in some dingy town
to stay in its only hotel,
where my little sister cries all night from bites
while Mother hunts bedbugs
scooping them from the wall
into the glass shade of an oil lamp.
Her shadow, huge, moves along the walls.

In the morning we are picked up
by a peasant with a horse-pulled wagon
lined with hay-stuffed cushions,
the best part of the trip.
On the way to my aunt's farm
we pass fields swaying with ripening wheat,
farmhouses where storks built their broad nests
and an old forest, 'puszcza,'
where a nighthawk, imprisoned in a huge cage,
calls out with longing and despair.

My aunt's farm swarms with kittens, piglets, calves.
The nearby puszcza swarms with mushrooms.
To this day the smell of cow manure

and the woodsy smell of mushrooms
carry the bittersweet of childhood.

As we grew older we rebelled against these migrations
into the eastern townships.
Other trains, other places:
ancient Kazimierz, Rybienko,
from where, on the first day
of September, 1939,
we caught the last train to Warsaw,
just as the war was starting.

Cattle trains.
Cattle trains carry secrets.
They have no windows
just slits between the boards.
Through these slits I look out at the countryside
and watch for signs of life, of freedom.

A teenage couple walk through the fields.
They hold hands, laugh.
They seem to be in love, they are free.

Inside the dark wagon
the sunlight throws stripes of light
on dark shapes of women covering the floor.
My mother and my two sisters among them.
Soon these bright stripes on their dresses
will be replaced by the blue and white stripes
of prison garb.
I try to hear what they are saying
but words get lost in the hum of prayers, cries, laments.
I turn to the slits to look for signs of hope.

The train heads southwest.
At the end of this journey
no friendly peasant with his horse and wagon,
no kittens, no woolly lambs,
no mushroom picking in ancient forests.

> The names of towns we pass inform us
> that our journey will end by the iron gate with a sign:
> *'Arbeit Macht Frei'**

My mother was consumed by fears of what had become of our father and brother. Last time we saw them was in the prison yard, where all of us were gathered before being taken by trucks to the railway station. The men were ordered to leave their shoes behind, and seeing them with their bare feet, looking so helpless and so vulnerable, seemed a very bad omen, although we discovered later on that the reason for it was an earlier incident – in another transport, some prisoners had kicked out the boards of the car's floor, and many had escaped through the holes.

When I heard that our destination might be Auschwitz my thoughts flew to my beloved Jerzy. At Gestapo headquarters, we had to face the wall while waiting for the interrogation. There was a map of Poland in front of my eyes. I found Auschwitz, and I wished that if we were to be sent to a camp, let it be Auschwitz. My silent wish would be granted. Knowing that he was in there made the place very desirable for me – I wanted so much to be near him. He would soon find out about our arrival. Would I be able to catch a glimpse of him? What did he look like by now? I knew that he was alive, for he was writing letters home. He was sent there in November 1942, some six months before us. Arrested at a secret meeting at Urszula's. She and her mother were also arrested and sent to Auschwitz. Were they alive? Would I see them?

We were on our way. But the four of us were together and Father and Tytus were on the same train. I don't recall how many of us were in this cattle car, but it was crowded, sitting room only on the filthy floor covered with bits of straw. In the corner, a stinky bucket. Some women were crying, some were praying out loud, and still others were speculating on our fate.

I would get up, once in a while, to look at the world through the cracks between the wooden boards of the car. As we were passing some fields, there was a path between them, and along the path walked a teenage couple holding hands, laughing – in love. That sight made me realize, more passionately than ever before, that we were

---

*'Work Sets You Free.'

heading towards another world – a world where death and hate triumphed over life and love. And yet, a sense of inner freedom, even then, allowed me to realize that no one could take away my thoughts, my hopes and my love, no matter how sick I might be, how hungry and how helpless I was made to feel in my external existence. I don't believe I ever lost this conviction during the following two dark years, and maybe this inner immigration, plus my capacity to daydream, enabled me to survive those cruel months.

Finally we arrived at our destination – Auschwitz, as we had guessed from the names of the towns we were passing. It was a beautiful, balmy night on 13 May 1943. As the cattle-car doors were being opened, a wave of fresh air filled our lungs. Its impact was almost intoxicating after hours of being confined in this hot and stuffy car, with a bucket full of excrement in the corner exuding a heavy, sickening odour.

Yes, we were in Auschwitz, or rather in Birkenau, Auschwitz II – the women's camp and also, as I found out later, the gypsy camp, as well as a section of the men's camp.

We got off the ramp. We were led by an SS-woman to a lit-up entry, a sort of gate, where I spotted a bush of white lilacs, in full bloom, lit by the meagre light from a naked bulb. This sight was most heartening. I carried in my heart a silent conviction – where there were flowers blooming, nothing bad could be happening. My two sisters seemed to share this idea with me. But soon this naive and romantic notion was shattered by the guards shouting and pushing us: 'Raus, Raus! Schnell, Schnell! Aber schnell.'

We were led to a block and ordered to line up. There were tables along the block wall, lit up by electric bulbs, and young women prisoners were sitting behind the tables. They all wore a yellow Star of David sewn on the top left side of their prison dresses. They seemed to be absorbed in some function that became clear when my mother's turn came and she was told to roll up the sleeve of her left arm. I watched as she was submitted to this mysterious procedure first – the girl on the other side of the table was printing something on my mother's left arm. I was next, and the prickle of a sharp needle touched my skin. She was using a sort of fountain pen, with a very sharp needle that drew the number with many tiny pricks, and the ink flowed into the tiny holes. She was printing my number: 44787. My mother's was 44786.

My mother despaired on our behalf: how would we ever be able to wear sleeveless ball dresses with this terrible tattoo on our arms? She was not here yet – in her mind she was still living in the world that had not existed for us for the last four years. Or she was projecting her thoughts into a future that might never come to us. Oh, sweet Mother of three young daughters. Our debut is tonight: we're going to fashion the latest in prison garb, the striped, blue-and-white prison dresses, with lice and nits in their seams. Marina was next to me, and her number was 44788, then Zosia, 44789. This detail of initial degradation was not known to me until this moment. There was a sense of dread in the air, and it increased with every moment as we were submitted to the horrible procedure through which all the new prisoners had to go.

Step by step we were being deprived of all the external signs of identity, step by step we went through degrading and dehumanizing rituals.

After the branding
we stripped off our 'freedom' clothes
to submit our bodies to shearing:
blond braids,
dark curly bands,
glimmer of silver,
spattering of pubic hair collected
into ghastly mounds
on the stone floor of the 'sauna.'

Stripped of our outer selves
we were chased through the cold showers
by the Mephisto voice of a prisoner-whore
brandishing a wooden club,
her magic wand of terror, over our Matisse bodies.
Her shouts fell like heavy blows
on our naked shoulders, breasts, thighs,
still unblemished by the bites of vermin, by the bite of hunger.
We were given stiff prison dresses,
white kerchiefs to cover our ravaged heads.
A strange order of nuns:
schoolgirls, mothers, grandmothers,
a captured Army of the Resistance.

Our parents brought us up to guard our privacy most diligently. This puritanical attitude had very grave reasoning: we lived in rather congested conditions. Our apartment in Warsaw consisted of four bedrooms, a salon, a dining room, and a kitchen with a small alcove. Marina, who was two years older than I, shared a bedroom with me. My parents had their own bedroom, and so did my brother. The fourth bedroom was Father's study. Zosia, my younger sister, slept on a couch in the salon. Grandmother and Aunt Lucia shared the small alcove by the kitchen. The maid used to open up her portable cot every night in the kitchen. In this rather crowded household, the unspoken rules of privacy prevailed.

Even though I shared a bedroom with my sister Marina, we never saw each other's naked bodies. To undress we would turn away from each other, respecting the sacredness of this unspoken rule. Even during our six-week stay in Pawiak prison, we guarded this rule of modesty and dressed and undressed with our backs to the other prisoners.

Now all this was being shattered traumatically and we were exposed to one another's nakedness. Our young bodies, even though depleted during our six weeks in the prison, still retained some of their healthy appearance. Suddenly, shame left us, and we didn't seem to be weighed down by that pre-disaster modesty. Something more powerful was happening around us, and these 'normal' attitudes didn't have a place here. What I recall was a feeling of deep compassion towards my mother and sisters, and towards myself. Gradually we were all made equal, with no hierarchy of age, no seniority. We were face to face with death – equally.

By the time morning came, we were all done, transformed. We did look like nuns of some strange order: our shaved heads covered in a uniform fashion with a white cotton triangle, tied neatly and tucked in at the nape. Coarse underwear, tied with a drawstring – one size fits all. We were given wooden clogs that felt awkward and rough on our bare feet. Stiff prison dresses completed our outfits.

On the top left side of the dresses, where the heart was, sewn-on white cotton labels bore our prisoner numbers and a red triangle signifying 'political,' with a letter 'P' for Poland.

Sad years, take me.
Gather me into your cool and distant shade
as I dream and weep
as I weave grief-wreaths, crowns of thorns.
Grass doesn't grow in Hades, flowers don't bloom.
Step gently, young Ariadne.
Surrounded by living shades you grope in sleep-like daze.

Your wooden clogs sink deep into this foul clay,
while your astonished heart sings Niobe's sad lament.

Thick air, dark.
The sun won't reach the earth today.
This flaming pyre –
dumb chimney's spouting snout –
Humanity's Dies Irae.
What words, what metaphors
what tongue can undertake
to sing this dark Requiem.

Pitiful Ariadne,
don't let go your precious thread
its pure skeins strong, sturdy:
Faith, Hope and Love,
with power to set you free
although your captive body
is branded, starved and sick.

We were led to block no. 2. It was supposed to be a quarantine block where we would stay for some time. It was actually a horse stable transformed into a dwelling for prisoners. It was meant to contain fifty-two horses. Now, it housed close to a thousand women prisoners – the stalls were filled with three wide shelves that could accommodate several bodies each. Dark blankets covered a layer of straw. Through the centre of the stable ran a low brick wall. It turned out that it was heated by the fire burning at the front and at the back of the wall. The warm air from the fire warmed up the bricks.

The four of us settled down on the middle shelf. It would save us climbing up after a day in the fields. Today, we were exempted from going to work.

After we'd staked out our territory, we heard someone calling our names. It was a tall girl who looked vaguely familiar. She introduced herself as Urszula. Yes, I knew her from Warsaw. She and her mother were arrested last November at a secret meeting at their home, together with Jerzy and some other members of their Resistance group.

Arrested five months before,
Urszula came to greet us in our quarantine block.

Gathering stiff folds of her prison dress
she sat on a lower bunk and told us her story.
She and her mother,
reduced to skeletons by typhus,
were on the truck to the gas chamber.
The snow was high.
She slid into its white cover
and crawled back to her block.

A thin rivulet of saliva
trickled from her mouth,
down her chin, while her hands
travelled up and down her calves.
'The vermin,' she explained.

Through the block window's dirty panes
the sun threw golden light
onto the clay floor.
The sky filled with red and golden hues.
Against reason,
faith, hope and love flooded my being.

Urszula represented a model of what might become of us. However, she also comforted us with a bit of information aimed at decreasing our anxiety – she told us that as of March 1943 the political prisoners, even if they were too emaciated to work after an illness, were not to be sent to the gas chamber but were allowed to recover and to return to work. At that time I was not able to appreciate sufficiently the importance of this new regulation to our survival.

But how did this new rule come into being? There were rumours that there was a well-organized Resistance movement in Auschwitz, but it was only after the war that I could grasp the significance of their activities. These included facilitation of prisoners' escapes by providing false documents and places of hiding. Those prisoners who worked in camp offices passed on information to the Resistance. Documentation of crimes and names of the main SS criminals were passed on to the civilian population outside the camp and, through it, to London and the British Broadcasting Corporation. This worried the camp command, especially when the war situation pointed to Hitler losing the war. I often wondered if these pressures had forced the camp command to stop the gassing of sick political prisoners who, in terms of war, were soldiers of the Army of the Resistance.

Later I found out that Jerzy also had typhus in December and, like Urszula, was also designated for the gas chamber. However, at the last moment an SS-man asked him what his profession was. Jerzy replied that he was a mechanical engineer. He really wasn't yet, but before his arrest he had been studying to become one at a secret university in Warsaw. The SS-man moved him to the other side, where those to be saved stood. What did Jerzy feel during these minutes between being condemned and being saved?

After telling us her story, Urszula informed us that Jerzy was in Auschwitz I, the main men's camp. Then she left us, so we could get some rest before tomorrow's ordeal. At supper time we got our small rations of dark bread and some warm herbal tea. We covered ourselves with the flea- and lice-infested blankets and slept, gradually getting accustomed to our communal bed of hard wooden boards.

Next morning, at dawn, we were awakened by loud shouts and a lot of commotion in the block. There was no water to wash with, but there was a pail to empty our bladders into. We had no other needs, as we hadn't eaten for forty-eight hours, except for the ration of bread the previous day. There was no hair to bother with – we tied our white kerchiefs at the nape of our necks. Our dresses looked creased because they also served as our nightgowns. I examined the bites from the fleas. No use counting them – there would be more as time went by. Some warm herbal tea was ladled out into our tin cups – our breakfast.

We went out into the fresh May dawn and lined up in front of the block for the roll-call. We learned from other prisoners that this procedure might last an hour or two, depending on how quickly the Germans counted all the prisoners in front of all the blocks. Thousands of them. If no one escaped in the last twenty-four hours, the roll-call wouldn't be too long. If, however, one person was missing we would stand there forever.

We were not allowed to talk. I didn't know about this rule and turned my head to my mother to say something. A young Jewish prisoner, who acted as a helper (*Stubendienst*) to the German prisoner in charge of our block (*Blokälteste*), ran up to me and slapped my face. My mother was enraged and ready to yell at her, but I held onto her and said that I was all right. I believe that the girl was more scared than we were, and she had to act tough to keep her job as her boss was keeping an eye on her. At first I was furious – no one had ever slapped my face – but later, in my heart, I forgave her.

After a couple of hours of roll-call, our legs tired of standing, we were told to line up for work. There were five of us in each row. It was the first time since we'd arrived that we were walking along the main street, towards the gate.

To our immense surprise, an all-female band stood by the gate, playing a jaunty tune, 'Erika.' The ensemble was led by a supposedly famous Hungarian violinist, Alma Rose. And so, to this tune, we marched out, feeling glad to stretch our legs while we watched the unfolding countryside. The shouts of the SS-men and the monotonous call *'Links, Links, Links, und Links'* (meaning 'left') accompanied us right to Rajsko, where there were ditches to dig and gardens with rows of cabbages and other vegetables to weed.

Our *Kapo* wore a black triangle – a German whore. She had broad, peasant features, and her voice was hoarse. She treated us with disdain, as befitting a member of Hitler's superior race, even though in her country, as a prostitute, she belonged to the lowest social stratum.

We passed the gate and the barracks occupied by Mandel, the commandant of the women's camp, Birkenau, and a tall SS-woman named Drexler. She was nicknamed 'Death' by the prisoners because her mouth never closed over her protruding teeth.

We were marching under the command of the SS officer. There were also many guards with rifles, accompanied by the ever-present German shepherd dogs. But even though the ugly sound of the oppressor's brutal language accompanied us all the time, and heavy work awaited us at the end of this march, we were thrilled by the fresh greenery of the meadows, by the birds singing above us, by the softness of the road under our feet. We filled our lungs with fresh air, free of the foul stench of the camp, and full of the intoxicating scent of wild flowers.

Our Polish companions were familiar to us as we had spent six weeks with some of them in the cells at Pawiak prison. My sisters and I were the youngest members of this group. Mother talked to the other prisoners about her concerns, about Father and our brother, who were in the main camp, Auschwitz I. I was lost in a reverie about Jerzy, and as we passed columns of male prisoners, I watched every passing row looking for his face.

In the fields we were afraid of 'White Neck,' so nicknamed because of a white bandage around his neck. No one knew the reason for the bandage. He appeared suddenly, on a motorcycle, and scrutinizing the situation, he always found a victim for his fury. Mercilessly, he would throw her on the ground and kick her violently. She would never be able to return to this work again.

We were not allowed to stop the work of weeding, never allowed to sit or kneel down. Nonetheless, we were determined to maintain the speed of tortoises, to preserve energy, to preserve our lives. When we first arrived in this accursed place we were ready to do as we were told, to 'work hard' to avoid punishment. How quickly we caught on to this 'work slowly' formula! And if any of the prisoners forgot it, carried away by a lifelong habit of working diligently, other prisoners would stop her, asking: 'What are you doing? Are you in a hurry for the chimney? Slow down, you crazy woman.'

That first spring in Birkenau there were many rainy days, but we had to carry on as usual. One rainy and chilly day we were walking back to the camp, after working in Rajsko's vegetable patch, where we had spent a wet and cold day, up to our elbows in mud, trying to weed some cabbages. Suddenly, we heard Zosia's loud and pitiful crying. Mother asked her if she had hurt herself or whether she was cold. Zosia said, still sobbing loudly, that it was nothing in particular. She was suddenly overwhelmed by our terrible fate, and she was crying in frustration and anger 'at those terrible Germans who are treating us so badly.' Her crying expressed, for all of us, what we felt on that cold and dreary morning.

Another morning, the rain was so fierce that our column stopped to seek shelter in an old, bombed-out house by the road. On its wounded walls sat a tattered roof, full of holes. A wild bush of charlock, planted by the wind, occupied the top of the stove. Raindrops splashed heavily on its broad leaves. The air was warm and steamy from our soaked dresses, and we were happy to have this moment of respite. Next door, in the part that was better protected from the rain, our *Kapo*, the SS guard, and the *Aufseherins*, the women overseers, talked and laughed loudly.

As we were snuggling up to one another, my mother, sad and melancholy, asked me to sing Schubert's 'Ave Maria.' I sang, with tears in my voice, words describing the suffering of a mother as she watched the suffering of her son. Everyone was in tears as my light soprano voice flew up to the cloudy sky and trembled in the rain-filled air. Even the loud voices in the room next door suddenly grew silent. By the time I finished my prayer-song, the air was full of cries and loud sobbing.

6
No Lilies for Mother

A messenger came from the gate one day with news that Zosia was to be transferred to what we called the 'freedom' quarantine. Of course, we didn't know whether she'd be released or moved to another camp or sent back to Pawiak in Warsaw. We speculated about it for hours, hoping that, because of her young age for a political prisoner, she would be released. After a couple of weeks at the quarantine, deloused and less emaciated – she was given milk daily and a larger ration of bread – she was sent away. We couldn't know about her fate – and yet we were glad that she was released from this Auschwitz hell.

On rainy days, as we had no change of clothes, we had to wear our wet dresses on our bodies both day and night. This might have led to my mother's illness. One day she developed a cough, accompanied by a pain in her chest and a fever. After long debates, it was decided that she couldn't continue working. Next morning she stayed in the block and was later escorted to the camp hospital. Because we were still in so-called 'quarantine,' we were not allowed to enter the rest of the camp, and so we were not able to visit Mother in the hospital.

My brother Tytus, who worked with Father in their camp's building office, joined the *Kommando* of carpenters who came daily to Birkenau to do some work on the blocks. In this way he was able to visit Mother every day. The men prisoners seemed to have far more freedom in our camp than the women prisoners.

These were the most horrible times when I felt an overwhelming despair. Thanks to Marina, who seemed to be stronger and very supportive, I was somehow managing. Not being able to visit Mother was most frustrating, although I knew that she was still alive.

Every day, after work, I went towards the main road dividing our block from the rest of the camp. It was there that sometimes I would get a chance to see my brother, after his visit to the hospital, and he would give me reassuring news about Mother.

One day, on the other side of the road, I saw my brother. He was in a terrible state, crying loudly, like a little boy. Through his sobs, he managed to tell me what had happened. When he got to the hospital, Mother was not there. He was told that she had died at night, her body carried out and laid on top of other bodies, outside the block. In the morning, the bodies were picked up by a truck and taken to the crematorium. And so we were walking and crying on the opposite sides of the camp's main road.

How did I cope with this terrible loss? Years later I came upon a book called *Dying* by Tor-Björn Hägglund. In discussing the role of 'inner' and 'outer' objects in mourning, he argues that to endure the immediate reactions to object loss – such as intense psychic pain and grief, attachment to the object, and aggressive feelings caused by frustration – requires a good inner object and even a good, contemporary external object.

Reading these words helped me understand how I was able to cope and go on, even after this devastating loss. My good internal object – my beloved Aunt Lucia – was in my thoughts to the extent that I almost believed she was hovering over me, like a guardian angel, protecting me from evil. My sister Marina was with me all the time, and though also of course weakened by this loss, she seemed stronger and even more supportive of me. And then Jerzy was there as well, just three kilometres away, thinking of me and loving me.

Mother

Dark eyes gaze sadly
from a photograph
the only picture that survived
thousands of miles of time
decades of space

You were sixteen then
Ahead of you

a lifetime of struggle
woven into two wars' dark tapestry
rich with love and sorrow

Your hands rest
on an empty planter or a crib
Photographer's enigmatic prop
symbolizing absence of life in both

Your hands' cool touch
on my burning forehead

Your hands gather my face
wet with tears of life's first hurts

Your hands smooth my hair
plait scrawny pigtails of childhood

Your hands – scent of wild flowers
woodsy smell of mushrooms

Your hands – bright torches
guiding my way through darkness

I remember Mother talking about her fear of being buried alive. She used to imagine that a doctor might make a wrong diagnosis and proclaim her dead. It was not really clear how it would happen, but the fear existed, and whenever she talked about her death she imagined being buried alive. By the time she would regain consciousness, it would be too late – the lid of the coffin closed, the coffin lowered into the grave. What horrifying pictures her imagination wove: in a closed coffin, at the bottom of the grave, she hears handfuls of earth being dropped on the satin-lined lid, her muffled cries unheard by those above who sing hymns offering her soul to God. I guess that such terrible incidents could have happened, once in a while, in some small villages in eastern Poland, and as a child Mother must have created, in her vivid imagination, this claustrophobic fear that accompanied her into her mature years.

It happened differently for her: she died on a hard, wooden hospital bunk bed, and her body was gathered in the morning, with others, onto a truck and offered to the fires of the crematorium.

No lilies, no asphodels, no funeral rites: the wind scattered your ashes to play with the stars.

7

Gifts and Secrets

Every morning I woke up with terrible hunger. The herbal tea did not appease it, and the watery nettle soup at lunchtime didn't erase the great hunger gnawing at my innards. It took time to adjust to life on these meagre rations. Every morning I promised myself that in the evening I would eat only half of the bread ration we received for supper – about 200 grams. Sometimes a spoonful of beetroot jam was added, and on Sundays we would even get a piece of sausage, about 20 grams.

One evening I managed to deprive myself and save half of my bread ration for this long-awaited treat at breakfast. I placed the bread under my head and fell asleep, smiling with anticipation of the next morning when I would have a feast.

Next morning I woke up with a vague sense of something pleasurable awaiting me. Sudden awareness, a sleepy and hazy memory, made me reach for the bread. It was not there. Gone. It was a hard moment. I was overcome by a mixture of anger, self-pity, and bewilderment. Did the thief watch me place my bread under my head? Did she come in the middle of the night and take it while I was deep in sleep? How could she? Maybe she routinely checked, every night, if others still as naive as I was hid half of their ration under their heads for their breakfast?

Gradually I learned one terrible truth: some prisoners would do anything to survive. But how could anyone hope to be nourished by a piece of stolen bread? Surely their soul would be gradually destroyed, and with it their body too. Maybe some people didn't feel guilt even if they stole. Slowly, painfully, I learned about these hard realities.

Another incident, less traumatic, occurred during this period. I was getting up one morning, feeling with my feet for the familiar touch of my wooden clogs. I could locate only one. The other was gone. What was I to do? Go to the fields with one shoe on? I kept looking for it frantically, even though everybody had left for the roll-call. Finally, a victory! There was the other clog. But to my despair, it was from the same foot. Two left clogs were better than one, so I put it on. All throughout the day, each time I looked at my feet, I couldn't help but smile. I looked like some tragicomic female Charlie Chaplin, doing a left-foot act.

I never realized how hard it would be to get used to being a living feeding-station for vermin, the constant companions of our nights and days. After a while a bloody belt formed around my waist, which would not heal. Even if I tried not to scratch during my waking hours, at night my hands would tear again at the bloody scars. Both fleas and lice were our constant curse. At lunch breaks I tried to catch the lice in the seams of my sweater and kill them between the nails of my thumbs. They were large and transparent – their little bellies filled with my blood, which splashed and covered my nails. Once, I counted one hundred. I worried mostly about developing further infection in my bloody belt, but fortunately it didn't happen. On that count I was glad that we had no hair on our heads to provide a home for head lice.

One day our block was left half-empty as the whole lot of prisoners – all those marked with numbers starting with 43,000 (ours started with 44,000) – ended their period of quarantine and were moved to the regular blocks.

Soon afterwards, the block filled up with the shrill voices of new young prisoners and the screaming of the *Stubendienst*. The *Zugangen*, or newcomers, wore khaki pants and shirts, which were marked with a thick red line on the back. These outfits were leftover uniforms of the Soviet prisoners who'd died since coming here in October 1941.

The newcomers wore multicoloured scarves that covered their shaved heads – their faces had dark complexions, soft features, and black, gentle eyes framed by long, black lashes. Their language was different from other Auschwitz dialects. The Jewish girls from Saloniki, like Feuchtwanger's Jewess from Toledo, talked in a dialect that the Spaniards would recognize as archaic Spanish, used at the time when the Inquisition was getting rid of the Jews in Spain and many of them ended up in Greece. The Germans had occupied Greece and were transporting the Jews to Auschwitz. Many of the girls spoke French as well. Most of them were daughters of merchants, and their stories about white villas on the shores of Greek islands, the azure sea, and the Mediterranean sun added a romantic and dreamy element.

Marina and I were enchanted by these exotic beauties. Despite their old khaki uniforms, they looked to us like movie stars. These girls were told that this place was just a stopover before they would be moved to a proper resettlement camp. In the evenings they danced and sang, totally unaware of the horror of this place.

As time went on they gradually lost their vitality. Many of them fell prey to malaria; others died of typhus. Most of them perished because of illness and the harsh conditions in the cold and damp climate.

Once in a while we received a small food parcel from Jerzy. Sometimes it contained some salami; at other times he sent a chunk of cheese. These packages arrived via men prisoners who came to Birkenau to work as carpenters. We were incredibly grateful to Jerzy for these gifts, as hunger was so hard to endure. Often, there was a loving note inside the packet, to his 'Dear Girls.'

These gifts made me think of others that I had I received from him, the gifts that remained in my memory – not material objects but his help. In my high school there was a dreaded physics teacher. She was tiny, and her nickname among the students was 'The Pip.' She couldn't tolerate those girls who were not able to grasp the laws of physics. She was quite sadistic towards her poor, bewildered victims. She would reduce them to babbling idiots who were not able to tell her on how many legs her desk stood. I dreaded her, and I was determined to conquer all the material that she taught so she wouldn't be able to do the same to me.

Jerzy, after hearing my horror stories, decided to tutor me in physics. I was immensely grateful, as he made it all so clear for me. We used to meet whenever possible, at my home, and we managed to cover the whole second-year program within weeks. For once I was sitting in Pip's classes relaxed and confident that if she asked me a question I would give her an answer that was clear and correct.

The summer that followed the first year of occupation had been a busy one for us. The Germans established a rule that all students had to have a job during the summer vacations. Here my English teacher,

Klara Jastroch, came to the rescue. She owned some plots of land in a Warsaw suburb, and she decided to turn them into vegetable gardens. She employed her students to work as part-time help there.

That summer Jerzy was determined to teach me to swim. My fear of water had been with me since I was about three. We lived then in Brzesc, and sometimes the whole family would go to the nearby beaches of the Muchawiec River. Mother was a good swimmer, but Father couldn't swim at all. Once Mother had me hold her neck with my hands and she swam out with me far away from the shore. At one point I let go of her neck and grabbed her shoulders, making it impossible for her to move her arms. I don't know how she managed to swim with me to the shore, but from that time on I retained a fear of water and of swimming. Jerzy was determined to help me get over that fear.

We developed a busy schedule. We got up at five in the morning, met around six at the streetcar stop, and travelled to a little lake, called Czerniakowskie Lake. After the swimming lesson we returned to the city – he to his practice at the Vavelberg School, I to my weeding in Klara Jastroch's vegetable gardens. One day, near the end of the summer, Jerzy brought his father with him, and we went together to the lake. It was a lovely, warm August morning. His father, being a physician, was allowed to own a car in those hard days of the occupation, and we travelled this time in luxury. We passed the grim Warsaw suburbs, and soon we saw our lake. On one side there was a row of young birches; on the other there was a meadow covered with wild flowers, mostly white daisies. A bridge ran across the lake. When we reached the shore we shed our outer clothes – we wore our swimsuits underneath. I wore my navy-blue swimsuit, in which I looked very slim, and my skin was golden-brown from working in my teacher's gardens. Jerzy's tall, muscular body gleamed in the early morning sun. He suggested that the two of us swim across to the other shore. I had not done this before, but I felt that if he was confident I could do it, then I would not disappoint him. And so we swam, while his father watched us from the shore. It was wonderful to see how proud and happy Jerzy was when we reached the other side. He hugged me exuberantly, showing his pride in me. After a brief rest, we swam back to his father. This gift of swimming I've retained all my life.

At the end of the summer we received a modest wage for our work in Klara Jastroch's gardens. Elated, I took my money to a tobacco store to buy cigarettes for Aunt Lucia. She was a heavy smoker. She rolled her own cigarettes, as she couldn't afford to buy ready-made. I asked the shopkeeper for the most luxurious cigarettes that he had. He suggested the Egyptian ones. I bought a package and hurried home to present them to my aunt. To my great dismay, she was upset. She pointed out that for the money I had spent she could have bought enough tobacco to last her for a couple of weeks. I guess it was a bitter lesson in empathy for me. Had I possessed the ability to put myself in her position, I would have thought of asking what kind of treat she would have liked best.

I had also wanted Jerzy to help me with my English studies. His high school, like mine, offered English in addition to the usual French and German, and he had been studying English for the past six years. Because of illness, I was a few days late starting my first year of high school. I was also late that first morning of the autumn term. While the other students were in their classrooms, as the lessons were about to commence, I was wandering the long corridor, wondering where my class might be. Fortunately, one of the teachers appeared in front of me. She bent down and spoke in a gentle voice, asking me which first-year class I was supposed to be in. Seeing my puzzled expression, she explained that there were three first-year classes: one, where the foreign language was French, another for students studying German, and a third for those who chose English. Momentarily, I was caught unprepared for an instant choice, but then I reached a sudden decision: 'I'd like to study English,' I replied, remembering that Jerzy also chose this language at high school. One more thing to have in common with him.

The teacher beamed with pleasure. 'Then you'll be in my class,' she announced, and she opened a door to a room already filled with students. As we entered, all the girls stood up, and they stayed standing until Klara Jastroch nodded her permission to sit down. There was an empty seat next to a girl with freckles and long, dark-blond braids. Klara asked me my name and entered it in her register. She called me Helena, my given name, as did all the teachers.

Unlike Britain, where the work and school week generally had five days, Poland had six. Klara Jastroch was determined to introduce us to what she called 'English Saturdays' in a program she specially devised. She taught us English songs – one that comes to mind is 'My Bonnie Lies over the Ocean' – and we learned by heart many poems – the one that I remember best is 'My Heart's in the Highlands' by Robbie Burns. We looked forward to those 'English Saturdays.'

When I asked Jerzy to assist me with my English, he came up with another idea. He suggested his close friend, Jacek Tabecki, as my tutor. Jerzy claimed that Jacek's English accent was superior to his own. Jacek spoke English at home with his mother, a violinist who had travelled the world before the war with her recitals and knew a number of foreign languages.

Jacek agreed to tutor me, and we had several sessions during which I felt shy and uncomfortable, but also appreciative, because he sounded quite like those actors in the American films we used to see in the local parish cinema before the war. One day Jerzy brought the sad news of Jacek's arrest and his deportation to Auschwitz. At this point we were touched personally, for the first time, by the seriousness and gravity of our life and the dangers that surrounded us.

When even the commercial school in which we were studying was closed, I had to terminate my English-language studies as Klara Jastroch was charging a fee for private instruction. My father gave me a choice: to continue my piano lessons or my English studies – he couldn't afford both. I chose piano, for music has always been my love.

Even though we had no school to attend, we continued our studies in secret. Groups of five students were meeting all over the city, with their teachers, in the homes of either the students or the teachers. In Warsaw, by 1943, there were 2,118 teachers instructing 24,366 high school students, and 9,000 students were attending secret university lectures.

There were teachers who during the whole week never left their homes – giving lessons continuously to students – and there were teachers who from early morning until curfew rushed from one end of the city to another, by foot, by streetcar, up and down the stairs of countless floors, to give lessons and to get home before the curfew time.

The headmistress of my high school, Helena Kasperowicz, had this to say: 'The work of the teachers during the occupation was characterized by great sacrifices and by the decisive stand in the defence of Polish culture, endangered by the destructive policy of the enemy. Many women teachers tried to maintain contacts with the men teachers, deported to Germany, and these women paid with their life for their efforts.'

8
A Legacy of Herbs

While my mother was in the hospital, at Birkenau, she met one of the nurses, Rysia Wloszczewska, a young Polish woman who was there with her mother, a pharmacist. Rysia was concerned about her mother, as she was too feeble to dig ditches or work in the fields. The two of them conceived the idea of forming a *Kreuter Kommando*, a work group that would gather herbs for the hospital. Instead of aspirin – linden flowers, camomile, pansies, and bluebottles for other ailments. Everything for free: the fields outside the camp were covered with wild flowers, and twenty women prisoners would gather them daily, under Rysia's command. Her plan was approved by the hospital authorities.

When my mother heard of this plan, she begged Rysia to include Marina and me in this group. Rysia promised that she would, even though the main purpose of creating this *Kommando* was to provide light work for the elderly prisoners, like her mother. After my mother's death the plan was put into force and Marina and I joined the ranks of this distinguished group – professors, writers, teachers, and an actress from Wilno. They nicknamed us 'Infants,' as we were the youngest pair among these older women. We were thrilled and grateful about this miracle, which was the result of our mother's loving intervention. In our group was Professor Moszczenska. She, jointly with my high school teacher, Professor Mrozowska, had written history textbooks for high schools. Mrs Wloszczewska, Rysia's mother, was with us too, as it was to save her from hard labour that Rysia initiated this *Kommando*. Krystyna Wigura, with her elderly mother, and the beautiful actress Lusia Kielanowska were also among the group.

Every morning we marched out of the camp, with baskets on our arms, to gather field flowers in the meadows surrounding the camp.

The *Aufseherin* and the *Posten* (guard) treated us well, and if we found a patch of blueberries at lunchtime, we were allowed to linger until we were full of the fruit, our mouths dark from its juice.

One such lunch break we heard our names being called. We emerged from the little grove. Towards us were coming two men prisoners. One of them greeted us by our first names. He said that he was a friend of Tytus and Jerzy, and that we had met once in Warsaw, in our apartment. His name was Wojtek Kubasiewicz. We couldn't recall him, partly because of his shaved head and his prison suit. He and his companion were looking for marshes with mosquitoes, as their assignment was to do research on the insects, which were spreading malaria among the prisoners and the SS. They had one *Posten* assigned to them. Obviously there was also a certain amount of personal freedom in their job, as their *Posten* allowed them to chat with us.

We greeted Wojtek as a friend and sent our heartfelt greetings to Father, Tytus, and Jerzy. We learned from Wojtek that Father was working as an architect and Tytus as a draftsman in the Auschwitz I *Bauburo*, the building office. Now I learned that at the hospital where Jerzy had been sick with typhus, a doctor – a colleague of his father's from Warsaw – had taken Jerzy under his wing. After Jerzy had recovered, the doctor kept him working in the hospital, instead of releasing him to some other, harder work.

Seeing us in this blueberry patch must have made a positive impression on Wojtek Kubasiewicz, and we were glad that he saw us in this situation, rather than as bedraggled field workers. After he left, I saw in my basket, on top of the camomile blossoms, a packet. It contained a large sandwich of rye bread, spread thickly with lard. We had a feast, blessing our friend.

As we were gathering herbs that afternoon, there was a glad feeling in my heart – our encounter with Wojtek reassured me that our men were safe and healthy, and now they would be reassured about our not-so-terrible fate.

The Cherry Tree

It might have been late June, early July.
A sunny day.
We fill baskets with camomile, lavender, thyme,
for the camp hospital.

The fields sparkle with dew,
the last sounds of camp orchestra fade away
together with the stench of latrines,
helplessness and dying.
My companions
professors, teachers, writers
and an actress from Wilno – beautiful Lusia.
A cap of silver hair frames her suntanned face.
At midday breaks she recites
Ophelia, Desdemona, Electra.
Enchanted, I listen,
forgetting to hunt the lice.
Victorious, they evade
the 'click, click' of quick death
between my bloodied nails.

The countryside takes us gently in.
We breathe freer, fresher air,
a brief illusion of freedom.
I stretch and look around.
I see a cherry tree,
its branches heavy with ruby beads
against emerald splendour.

Mouths salivate, stomachs sing.
Hunger, the great equalizer:
professors, writers, teachers, students,
we run.

With quick, decisive jumps
she is ahead of us.
Her arm, in a commanding gesture,
tells us to halt.
She floats in a macabre dance,
her prison dress billowing.
Legs, in eager leaps, seem weightless
shoulders hunched up,
arms stretched in greedy gesture,
hands – grasping claws.

Her crooked fingers
reach out to heavenly boughs.

Greed! shouts her body.
Animal greed!

Dignity – the last weapon against our captors.
Its loss, our final defeat
Dignity, threatened by the wild beast, hunger.

We applaud in gratitude.
The tension broken,
we walk towards the tree.

Yes, hunger was with us always, and in this dramatic way, Lusia
made us aware of its power over us, and the following story illustrates
even more succinctly the importance of her role in our lives:

The cherry tree had hidden, mystical powers but this was known only
to Lusia, the Goddess of Dignity. As soon as she spotted the tree from
afar, she knew that she would have to act immediately, to save her
companions from degradation.

Not that the cherries had the power of the pomegranate seeds to
imprison them in this hell forever, as was the case with Persephone,
none of that. Far more subtle and insidious powers, however, were
involved here.

Actual eating of the cherries gave no other than the ordinary, sensual
pleasure of eating sweet, delicious fruit. What was of major, even
colossal, importance, was the manner of approaching the tree. Lusia
could predict it quite easily. She was familiar with these hidden mean-
ings in objects that were seemingly innocent. For what could be more
ordinary than a fruit-laden cherry tree, in midsummer, somewhere in
central Europe, in an old, deserted orchard? Yes, truly the tree was just
a tree. But it had the power to make these women forget, even temporarily, their dignity.

The danger here was inherent in these women's state of deprivation,
in their constant, humiliating hunger. Visions of food followed them
like demented furies. At times they tried to appease these furies by
exchanging long, flavourful descriptions of their favourite recipes –
sometimes even arguing fiercely about the details, about the ingredi-

ents. But hunger, that constant and cruel companion, had a hidden power over them. Lusia was well aware of this power, and she knew that the only way to deal with it was by gaining mastery over it.

For that power had an insidious and hidden quality: first, it would be the cherry tree, approached with animal greed – maybe even leading them to push each other out of the way to get the best-looking fruit; then, an animal-like devouring of their miserable portion of bread at the evening meal; and finally, in some horrid cases, even stealing each other's preserved portions from under their heads, in the middle of the night! And even worse! Here Lusia shuddered at the mere thought. There had been incidents of cannibalism in the camp: she could still see in her mind that skeleton, that shadow of a man, in a cage, placed on display for all to see – in his hand a human ear. He kept chewing it, oblivious to everyone.

But what if they ignored her pantomime and refused to look at themselves through her eyes? What if they continued running and behaving like hungry animals, ignoring their own and each other's dignity? Well, this was the chance she had to take.

They didn't disappoint her. They saw her acting out this unrestrained greed, saw her crookedly extended, clawlike hands, her elbows protectively pushing away possible rivals, her body hungrily shaking and twitching in a slow-motion run towards the tree. On seeing her in this pantomime they stopped, puzzled at first, but on recognizing their own, animal-like behaviour, they laughed and applauded: the animal was conquered, disempowered. They resumed their approach, but this time with pleasure and enjoyment, as if they had just finished a delicious breakfast and the cherries were an unexpected but welcome midmorning snack, on this fine July morning, in 1943, in Auschwitz II concentration camp.

Our *Kommando* sometimes ventured far afield, to many abandoned orchards and meadows. We might come across an apple tree, and then we would store apples in our baskets, under the camomile blossoms. We would share the fruit with friends who worked inside the camp.

One day we were assigned a not-too-bright guard. We turned into the road running along the wire fence of the men's camp. There we came to a strange wooden building, with windows blocked with wooden boards. Our guard hurried us along the road where a men's *Kommando* was working, filling up the ditch along the road with soft, grey dust. One of our companions, Krystyna Wigura, stumbled on a part of a human skeleton. We were gathering bilberry leaves in silence when the trees were shaken by the men we saw by the ditches, and a shower of small pears fell on us. The men were from the *Sonderkommando*, whose task was to service the gas chambers and the crematoria. They informed us that the sealed-up wooden building we passed was a temporary gas chamber, before the more efficient arrangements were built. A tall and handsome prisoner from France, whose name was Daniel, was telling us, while munching a pear, that he was brought here with his wife from France, where he worked as a tailor. His wife went straight from the ramp to the 'chimney,' while he was assigned to delegate others there.

'We're all sentenced to death,' he continued. 'After some time we'll be replaced by others. We just don't know when.' He pointed to his companions, who were chatting and laughing with the members of our group. 'Gallows humour,' he explained. 'These men hope that during their term the war will be over and they'll be saved.' We heard later that Daniel tried to escape when the liquidation of his group was imminent. He was caught and hanged. He died a bit earlier than his companions.

This encounter cast a dark shadow on this sunny day and many days that followed. A new awareness of the perverse cruelty of the Nazis hit me harder than ever. These good-looking, young Jewish men had to execute in the gas chambers hundreds, thousands, of their fellow Jews – men, women, and children – knowing that the same fate awaited them at the end unless the war ended during their service. If they survived, how would they live with that experience as part of their past? What cruel memories would haunt them until the end of their days?

We were told one morning that next day we were going to visit the main hospital in Auschwitz I, to deliver our herbs. My joy at the possibility of seeing Jerzy was marred by my waking up at night with a very high fever. But I was determined to go, and even though I felt weak, shaky, and shivery I managed to keep up with the group.

Finally, we were on the main *Lagerstrasse*, Auschwitz I. We walked towards a large brick building. At the entrance stood a tall, young prisoner, with a bright smile. Jerzy. While the members of our group were giving their baskets to some women prisoners who were to empty them in the hospital, he and I had a chance to exchange a few words. I told him that I was fine except for this terrible fever. I noticed that one of his upper side teeth was missing. I asked if it was from his interrogation. No, he lost it here. A quick and tender 'goodbye,' as a guard was approaching. In my basket – a sandwich.

Heather meadow in Kampinos Forest,
cobalt-blue sky of autumn.
Our hearts on fire – we didn't know that
a few months later we'd meet
on the main street of Auschwitz,
where you, at twenty-one,
a prisoner in the men's camp,
waited for my *Kommando* to pass by.
I, barely able to walk, my body on fire from typhus.
You – tall, handsome even in that prison garb.

It was easier to bear vermin, filth and cold,
illness, the terrible hunger, even the loss of freedom –
in my heart I was free – you were close by –
Birkenau to Auschwitz just a bit farther
than Marszalkowska to Krucza Street in Warsaw.
Awareness of your closeness sustained me:
eyes scanning grim columns of prisoners
always searching for you.
Wooden clogs seemed light, empty stomach felt full,
my heart filled with tender love for you.

I am writing my days – a tree shedding its leaves.
Carried by the wind they cover the heather meadow
while cobalt-blue skies look down forever.

9
High Fever

Next day I went to be admitted to the hospital. After I passed the crite-rion that legitimized me as a patient – a very high fever – I was led to a sauna, where I was given a cold shower and a long, rough cotton gown. I was then led across the camp, together with other patients, to the hospital blocks.

Inside one block I was directed to the lowest bunk, where there was already a young girl, suffering from *Durchfall* – a case of severe diar-rhoea. Needless to say, she was lying in her own excrement, but I was too ill to care. I slipped into the bed '*na waleta,*' which meant that my head was where her feet were, like the figures in a deck of cards. This was the usual way of sharing a bunk bed. Later I learned that I was sharing the bed with the young Anielka Gutt, daughter of a well-known Polish architect.

I didn't know how many days had passed. I was in a delirium when I saw a misty shape floating towards me. I was sure that it was an angel in a long, shimmering gown, bending over me and giving me a drink of water. The angel had Marina's face. It turned out that she, after I left, had developed high fever caused by some stomach disorder and, after going through the same admission routine, had found my hospital block.

Seeing me lying in my neighbour's excrement, she called a nurse and, after getting me cleaned up and changed, ordered that I be moved to a vacant middle bunk, where she joined me. In this mad place, if you had someone to speak on your behalf you were saved. If you were alone and without a voice, no one paid any attention. Marina also asked the nurse to wash and change Anielka.

For ten days I lay, usually unconscious, sweating profusely, because I was being treated for pneumonia. Jerzy had sent a doctor from his hospital to check me and to determine my ailment. I had typhus, but to keep me out of the infectious diseases block, where I'd be at risk of getting some other illnesses on top of typhus, the doctor declared that I had pneumonia and left some medicine to keep my fever down. Hence my sweating. In the middle of the night, Marina, like a true angel, helped me get my drenched nightgown off and gave me her dry one. She put on the wet nightgown, disregarding my typhus-carrying lice, and after drying it on her body, she dressed me in it again. She also made sure that I didn't dehydrate – there was always a cupful of water within my reach. It was a miracle that she didn't develop typhus.

As I lay next to Marina, most of the time I was totally oblivious to my surroundings. In my delirium I was transported to other worlds, to other times. Once I was a flower girl at my parents' wedding: I was floating on a cloud of white lilies that Mother held in her arms. Her young, smiling face was gazing lovingly at my young and handsome father. The air was filled with the scent of lilies and the song of a nightingale. Then, suddenly, it grew cold, and the snow was falling on the frozen lilies, on Mother's face. The bird song changed into the ringing of sleigh bells as we hurtled through the snow drifts, the fields covered with snow. The lights of the Minsk cathedral were shimmering brighter and brighter as we moved closer to it.

Then I was a young girl of seven, walking home from school in Milosna, the commuter town near Warsaw where we lived before we moved to the city. There was a ditch running along the road. In the ditch two young boys were calling me rude names. I didn't know them, and I was astonished at their meanness and at their totally mystifying need to hurt me. But as they moved closer I saw that they were wearing Nazi uniforms.

All of a sudden it grew dark, and I saw Mother's face – her cheekbones protruding, her cheeks sunken, and her eyes dark – huge black moons shining in her face.

I must have called out, for there was Marina's face bending over me and handing me a cup of water. After I moistened my parched lips I sank back into the world of strange dreams full of phantoms from the past. My whole grade-two class was crying as I recited the saddest poem that I had ever learned. The snowstorm was raging, the bitter wind was blowing, and I was a little girl asking the gravedigger to put me in my mother's grave, for my mother was in heaven now, and her grave was empty. The sadness was slowly relieved by my father's heroic tenor voice singing 'Lorelei.' It flowed into my dream and brought a sense of peace and safety, which I had always experienced at home when I heard him sing. These strange dreams ended after my fever decreased and I began to recuperate.

We heard one day that the infamous Dr Josef Mengele was going to do a selection in the nearby block no. 25, which contained only Jewish patients, most with infectious diseases. I'll never forget that night. As the selection was completed and the victims were loaded onto the truck, incredible screams and howls shattered the night and our hearts. These almost-inhuman screams penetrated my ears, my skull, and burrowed deep into my body. These cries rose to heaven, to the stars that shone down on the victims. Again, a powerful sense of helplessness overwhelmed me – this cruel, inhuman violence could have been our fate also had the camp regulations not changed just two months before our arrival. Urszula went through it with her mother, and so did Jerzy. Now the political prisoners were allowed to recover, gain strength, and return to their work – thus we were saved.

And here again I want to acknowledge the significance of Mother's loving intervention, which led to our working in the herb *Kommando*. We were able to preserve some modicum of strength, thanks to the light work, as well as to consume some vitamins in the berries and apples that we found in abandoned orchards while we were looking for herbs.

After ten days of high fever I started to recover. My recovery coincided with the arrival of the first food parcels from Warsaw, sent by Jerzy's mother. There was no one left at my home to send the parcels – neither my blind aunt nor my eighty-year-old grandmother was capable of doing it. Jerzy's mother had been sending parcels to him since the winter of 1942, and she'd learned what to put in them. These packages contained apples, onions, and garlic, and because of their content, nothing ever went rotten, unlike the cakes, bread, and other delicacies that other prisoners received. As well, onions and garlic had a very high exchange value. So, during these first days of convalescence when our stomachs were refusing the heavy dark bread, Marina used to trade some of the onions and garlic for white bread that other prisoners received in their parcels.

A message came one day – I don't recall by what means – that Jerzy was going to visit me. He was to join, for a day, the *Kommando* of carpenters that worked in our camp. I was still hopelessly weak, but I got up and leaned against my bunk bed, a shadow of the girl that I used to be, with my hair still short, wearing a long, coarse hospital gown, trembling with emotion while awaiting his appearance. After some endless time I saw his tall, slightly stooping figure coming towards me. We couldn't talk, but I could clearly hear, as he passed me, the words 'I love you.' These words breathed life into me.

Next to us were two Polish sisters, the same age as Marina and I, also recovering from typhus. Their morale was very low. It was visible in the row of stacked-up boxes on their bunk. The boxes contained rotting food – their illness prevented them from eating all of it. They didn't think of sharing it with the new prisoners arriving daily and starving on the meagre diet – those two complained bitterly that some Resistance fighters who lived in their building got into trouble with the Gestapo, which then arrested all the people on their floor. They were furious with the Resistance movement, in which they never participated. I felt truly sorry for them, and not because they felt unjustly punished. I felt sorry for them that they didn't belong to the Resistance. Being involved in the Resistance gave both Marina and me a sense of having actively defied the Germans. This stance had a powerful, lifting effect on our morale.

There was a young and pretty Polish girl on a bunk bed not too far away from us. We were quite taken with the short, blond curls that surrounded her round, peasant face. As we chatted with her, she told us that we were so foolish to work in the fields. She was very happy to work in a brothel in the men's camp. She serviced those prisoners who were exceptionally diligent in their work and could pay for her services with coupons they received as a reward. She volunteered for her work. She told us that she lived in a sweet little room, with curtains in the window and a real, comfortable bed, and she got good food. Marina and I looked at her with pity and wonder. Most probably, in her brothel, she was better off than she had ever been in some poor village in Poland. But why was she in the hospital? She was not too happy about this question. Finally, she reluctantly revealed that she was there to rest and to be cured of some infection she had received from one of her clients.

There were a number of new transports arriving from Pawiak prison, in Warsaw. Soon some of the newcomers found themselves in the hospital. While talking to them I discovered that Janek Bytnar, so bravely rescued by my brother and his companions, had died three days later. There had been no chance of saving him, as every organ in his body was damaged. One of the rescuers, Alek Dawidowski, also succumbed to the wound that he received during the rescue. He died on the same day as Janek.

This fatal news had to be kept from Marina. She never mentioned Janek, but I knew that in her heart she must have hoped he'd survived. And we all needed something to hope for, besides our own survival.

The newly arrived prisoners also told me that the secret underground press had published a book, *Stones for the Rampart*, written by Aleksander Kaminski, under the pseudonym of Juljusz Gorecki. This book described the story of the rescue and other stories from the Resistance activities in Warsaw. I also learned that, in revenge for the cruel torturing of the Resistance fighters, soldiers of the Resistance executed two of the Gestapo SS-men. One was an SS-man named Schultz, responsible for the department that carried out Janek's interrogation. He was executed one month after Janek's arrest. The other one, an SS-man named Lange, who carried out Janek's torture, was executed three weeks later, on 22 May 1943.

When I finally recovered some strength and Marina's stomach upset had diminished, we had to face the reality of going back to our block and also back to work in the fields. We were truly frightened at this prospect, as neither of us felt fit for hard physical work. We didn't know what had happened to the herb *Kommando*. Later on we found out that Rysia, who'd created this work unit to save her mother from hard work, had died of typhus. Her mother had died soon after her. Lusia Kielanowska, the beautiful actress from Wilno, also had succumbed to typhus during that summer of 1943.

We were barely out in the camp when Marina developed high fever, which we feared might be typhus. I was determined not to part from her. So both of us went for an examination, which by now we knew consisted mainly of taking our temperature. We were given a thermometer each, and she took her temperature with both. She gave me one that showed as high a fever as she had. We handed them in and were both admitted. Again, we shared the same bunk, and this time I took care of her.

At night I listened to the rats' feet making scratchy noises on the clay floor. Once, in the middle of the night, a woman screamed: 'It bites me, it bites me.' This horrifying moment I recalled in a haiku:

In the camp hospital
a rat nibbles
her still-warm toes.

After several days I realized that to stay with Marina I would have to be truly ill or find some work in the hospital. I heard there was a job as a nightwatch available, so I applied for it and got it. With each dawn began the dreaded routine of removing previous night's victims, previous night's messes. Shit and piss from overflowing buckets splashed on my legs and feet. During my duty only one prisoner died – an old woman suffering from blisters. Fat balloons of pus covered her skin. I prayed the disease wasn't contagious.

We stayed at the hospital over Christmas. My hair, before my illness, was starting to grow in. Now, because of typhus, it was falling out in handfuls. I retained a thin fluff of it, and on New Year's Eve I was nominated by the other prisoners to represent a baby New Year. We joked about my being such a skinny baby. We managed to cook some thin vegetable soup, using our onions and some potatoes that we obtained in exchange for garlic. How different from our beautiful, traditional Christmas at home.

On Christmas 1938 in Warsaw,
electric candles shone brightly
on green branches.
Every year the cat made her home
at the back of the manger.
It was warmed
by a light illuminating
the Holy Family.
Father built the manger himself,
thatched roof and all.
Under the starched white cloth
soft blades of hay on the big family table.
The table – another manger
in the centre, a blessed wafer – Christ's Body
shared by all the family before the meal,

and a spare setting for an unexpected guest,
in olden days lost in a snowstorm.

My grandmother
knelt down and prayed her thanks
for twenty years of Poland's independence,
a semblance of prosperity,
four healthy and beautiful grandchildren.
Grandmother broke the wafer,
sharing it with Mother, Father, all.
We wished each other Merry Christmas.

Twelve meatless dishes followed:
Herring in wine,
herring in sour cream,
Greek fish, Jewish fish,
carp in jelly, fried fish,
Russian salad,
mushroom flavoured
red barszcz with dumplings,
compote of dried fruit,
poppy-seed cake, honey cakes,
walnut torte – A feast.

Father opened the French doors
to the salon
and the cat scuttled from the manger.
The tree more splendid than the year before,
so many presents beneath,
so much joy.

When relatives from Krucza Street arrived
my heart danced mazurkas.
My seventeen-year-old cousin
whom I loved with all the passion
and tenderness of first love
gave me a bottle of cologne. Coty. *L'aimant.*
Christmas carols flowed from the radio:
'Lullaby my little Jesus, my little pearl,
Lullaby my little Jesus, my little pet.'

At the Church of the Redeemer
We celebrated Midnight Mass.

1938 – the last Christmas in free Poland.

My eyes were moist with tears as I wrote a long and patriotic letter
to my father, to Tytus, and to Jerzy. And so we entered the year 1944.

10
Designing a Dream House

Marina was slowly regaining her strength, and we knew that we would have to work outdoors again. However, one day a messenger came from the gate and announced that a new building office would soon be opened in Birkenau, and they were looking for architects, draftsmen, and secretaries – anyone with these skills could apply.

I begged Marina to put her name in, as she had been studying architecture, at a secret school, before our arrest. She refused to do so without me: 'We mustn't separate. No matter what, we have to stay together.' In my heart I agreed with her, but then I thought that if one of us was better off we would be winning by fifty per cent. She wouldn't accept my logic and insisted that I apply with her for the position of draftsman. She tried to convince me that, with my modest experience in Father's office and with her help, I'd be fine once we got the job. 'You know that this office is just a way of keeping some SS-men out of the Russian front. You know that there's hardly any building going on here,' she continued her reasoning. Finally she convinced me, and we went to apply.

We were interviewed by Mandel, one of the camp commandants in Birkenau, and an SS-man whom we identified as either an Estonian or a Latvian. All occupied countries, except Poland, had to produce divisions to strengthen the German army. I had a hunch that there was a romance between our interviewers, and Marina told me later that she had the same notion. We were convinced that Mandel was creating this *Kommando* in Birkenau to save her lover from death on the Russian front. At first we talked through an interpreter, but soon she was sent away – we spoke enough German to answer the questions.

As soon as the interpreter was gone the questions became more personal: why were we in Auschwitz? where were our parents? and so on. We were evasive about the first question, saying that it must have been some grave mistake, but we answered the rest: our mother died after the first few weeks in Birkenau – our youngest sister was sent away, we didn't know where – and our father and brother were both working in the building office in Auschwitz I. In a couple of days we learned that we were accepted as draftsmen.

My father loved his profession as an architect-builder, and he wished all his children would become architects. My brother was studying engineering – somewhat related to architecture. Marina had definitely chosen to follow in Father's footsteps. I was still undecided. My aspirations to become an opera singer had dissolved under the pressure of reality. When I was old enough for voice lessons the war broke out. My love of music found its expression in piano playing. Now I believe that I was saved from pursuing a career so full of anxieties and disappointments, even if I had a voice good enough to be successful.

During the occupation, regardless of which language we had studied before, we all had to take German while there was still a school to attend in the first couple of years. Later we did our high school program under the cover of a commercial school, but that too was closed. To sweeten the study of the German language, I found a way to combat my resentment: I played Schubert's *Lieder* on the piano and studied the German words of these songs. In this way I could accept the language of poetry and music.

When even the commercial school was closed, we continued our studies in secret groups of five, in our homes. Actually, it was a wonderful way to study. For the first time I participated eagerly in interesting discussions on a variety of topics. The teachers also enjoyed this close contact with their students, with our passionate views on history, politics, and literature.

Even though I didn't show much enthusiasm for architectural studies I was very fond of art and had spent many hours, when still in elementary school, painting watercolours. Father, who was also a great admirer of art, encouraged me and seemed pleased with my efforts. Needless to say, Marina was a very good artist and enjoyed Father's approval of her work.

When we were still quite young, Father used to take us to the Zacheta art gallery at least once a year. There he was, at the head of his family, who followed him like a flock of little ducklings, with

Mother closing the procession. I recall at some age, maybe nine or ten, feeling acute embarrassment when we had to look at the paintings that had nudity in them. There were some large canvases illustrating scenes from the novel *Quo Vadis* by Henryk Sienkiewicz. The book dealt with Roman times when the Christians were persecuted and thrown to the lions in the arena of the Colosseum. And there was naked Lydia, just about to be thrown to the lions. I remember my great discomfort at viewing this painting with Father in the same room of the gallery.

We were moved to block no. 4. The prisoners who worked in offices with the civilians or with the SS lived there. Therefore, they had to have access to better hygiene. We found out that we'd have a cold shower once a week. Such luxury! Up until this time, while we were in the field *Kommando*, we'd had to line up for hours on Sundays, for the water from a well, together with hundreds of prisoners. At the end, after several hours, all we could hope for was a metal bowlful of cold water.

The woman who was the head of our new block was a Polish political prisoner, Hanka. She was cheerful and friendly and complimented us on the healthy contents of our parcels. Soon we met the other members of our *Kommando*.

Our *Kapo* was the lovely and gentle Halina Von Shepping, a Polish architect from Warsaw. Another architect was Vera, a Jewish Czech from Prague, and her friend, also from Prague, was a secretary in our *Kommando*. Marina and I were working as draftsmen. There were two more Polish workers – Krysia and Genia. A young and pretty Hungarian Jewish woman also worked as a secretary.

Soon, to cover up my inadequacy as a draftsman, I developed a routine that was to protect me from being discovered: whenever an SS-man came into the room to check our work, I rushed to the wall pencil sharpener and busied myself with the pencils until all was clear.

There was a small iron stove in the corner of our room, and I was assigned the role of cook. Someone brought a few potatoes, someone else added some carrots and a chunk of margarine, and it was my task to produce a vegetable soup. At first I worried that the smell of cooking would annoy our bosses, but fortunately they had a habit of leaving at lunchtime. Sometimes I dropped a lid or a spoon and heard our Czech co-workers laugh: 'Ah, Lilka is cooking.' We got on so well with our co-workers. The two Czech women laughed at our Polish, saying that we sounded like little children. We got the same impression when they spoke Czech. After a while we developed a way of communicating, using a mix of the two languages.

At that time prisoners from the Theresienstadt Camp were being gradually transported to Auschwitz for systematic destruction. The transports started in September 1943. After each arrival, for several days the air was thick with ashes. We knew that Vera's mother was in that camp, located near Prague. In May 1944 she received a message that her mother would be in the next transport. The transport arrived in the evening. We sat with Vera all through that night, while her mother and hundreds of others were being gassed and cremated. Again, an overwhelming sense of horror descended on all of us.

Our *Kapo*, Halina, showed an almost maternal affection towards Marina and me. When the Gestapo had come to arrest her she had had to part with her five-year-old daughter. Her sister took care of the little girl, but this separation must have been very hard on Halina. Her husband also remained in Warsaw, hiding from the Gestapo.

Halina's concern for Marina and me was dramatically illustrated one day. Once in a while a civilian worker appeared in the men's *Kommando*. I think that he was a liaison between the office in Auschwitz I and our office. He was a good-looking Dutchman, always polite. His name was Van Marke. He wore civilian clothes.

One day Halina announced that because Van Marke had recently caught a venereal disease, all the members of our *Kommando* were ordered to have a medical examination. However, she added, because of our young age, she had begged to have Marina and me exempted. We were immensely grateful to her. After the examinations were completed, one member of our group was removed to the hospital. It was the attractive young Hungarian secretary.

In our block, in the adjoining room, there was the *Kommando* of men architects and draftsmen. Their *Kapo* was a German prisoner, Bernard. To prove himself to his bosses, he yelled orders at the top of his voice. But we all knew that at heart he was a gentle fellow, and the men were not afraid of his yelling. He had a green triangle, signifying a criminal. When, after some weeks, we asked him why he was in Auschwitz, he told us a tall story about having defrauded the Third Reich of one million marks. He could explain to the Gestapo only what he had done with half of the amount. He was imprisoned for not being able to account for the other half.

One day he came to our room and asked to talk to me privately. We went out into the corridor, and he, to my great surprise, asked me by what name my mother used to call me. I replied: 'Lilus' – a soft 's' at the end. He repeated several times: 'Lilush, Lilush.' I was puzzled, and returned to my work. Later the corridor resounded with a 'Lilush! Lilush!' I came out, and there he was, yelling my name. He handed me a broom and led me to the SS office. It was around lunchtime, and there was nobody there, as the SS-man Krug and his co-worker were out having their lunch in the SS canteen.

When we went inside, Bernard led me straight to the radio and turned the knobs. Suddenly I heard the voice of the BBC announcer, and on came the news in Polish. I was amazed and overjoyed – who would have thought? I listened attentively, and was suddenly aware of what an incredible privilege it was to be able to hear the news and to take it to our friends who were sick in the hospital and to other trusted prisoners in our block. It was 11 May 1944. The announcer said that the Allies were staging an attack on the Gustav Line, near Monte Cassino, in Italy. Within the next few days I heard that French North African troops had broken through the Gustav Line by crossing the Aurunci Mountains. On 18 May the Polish troops of General Anders captured the ruins of the monastery of Monte Cassino. I didn't have a map to locate all these places, but when I took the news to the other prisoners they explained some of the geographical details.

Every evening, as we marched into the camp, we were met by a number of friends, eager to hear about the war fronts. One of them was Severyna Szmaglewska. She was interested not only in the war operations, for she also had a friend in the male group of our office – a young architect, Witold Wisniewski – and I became a winged little cupid, carrying their love notes.

I suggested to Severyna that maybe one day she could take my place and join our *Kommando* so that she could visit her beloved. We went ahead with these arrangements, and I stayed with her *Kommando*, which worked inside the camp. Bernard was very helpful in this little romantic episode.

Years later, when I visited Poland in 1958 for the first time since my arrest and imprisonment, I visited Severyna. She was happily married to her Auschwitz sweetheart, Witold Wisniewski, and they had two young boys. Severyna, who was a journalist, wrote, soon after her liberation, a deeply moving account of her imprisonment, *Smoke over Birkenau*. In that first edition she mentioned my function as a cupid. (The second edition was a more impersonal account, more objective and reflective, with greater distance from her subjective experiences.)

On 4 June 1944 we were elated – the Allies had entered Rome – and on 6 June they invaded Normandy. Our morale was so high. Our hopes rose to the sky. News from the eastern front was also heartening: on 26 June the Soviets took Witebsk, and soon they regained Minsk and Wilno.

One noon hour Bernard and I listened to the news – after the Polish news from the BBC, a German version followed. Suddenly, we heard Krug's heavy footsteps in the hall. Bernard's face turned deep red as he turned off the radio, and I picked up a duster and busied myself at the shelves. Krug came in, mumbled something, and picked up some papers from his desk. In no time he had gone, and we wondered if he guessed our secret activity – or maybe, I hoped, he imagined that he had caught us in a romantic encounter, even though Bernard was at least twice my age. This would have been much safer. However, there were no repercussions, and after a few days Bernard and I carried on, as usual, with our secret activity.

Marina and I, having all the necessary means at our disposal, started to design, in our spare time, our dream house. Since Mother's death, Marina had become the oldest female in our family, and she was anticipating that once the war was over she would be taking care of all of us. Planning the house was great fun, and we indulged in this fantasy. It took us momentarily out of this place, into a future located in a cosy salon, with the fire burning in the fireplace, throwing flickering light on the faces of Zosia, Father, and Tytus. We designed our bedrooms with windows looking out onto a fine garden with rows of red and yellow roses, pink phlox, and dahlias of many hues. Aromatic scents of lilac and mock-orange bushes wafted, in summer, into our rooms. We were not sure in which part of Warsaw we would build this dream house, and this didn't worry us – maybe in a suburb, as Father, before the war, had bought some land outside the city. His plan was to leave a piece of land for each of his children. So we designed and dreamed.

Although my relationship with Marina had always been a warm one, our common experiences in the camp brought us even closer together. Here we were also free of the labels assigned to us by our family. Labels, if there were to be any, would now relate to character instead of being based on our temperaments.

When Marina was born Mother had realized that here was a child with a different personality – opposite to Tytus, who was a rather passive child, co-operative and polite. I believe that Marina was really more like Mother when she was little: full of spirit, determined to have her way, not wishing to be curbed and shaped into a person she was not. Even as a little girl, Marina led a stormy life: rebellious, assertive, her own little person. Mother tried to quash this power – having herself been brought up to submit to parental rule, she couldn't tolerate Marina's stubborn will. Marina was her daily reminder of the fire she had to suppress in herself. And the more Marina rebelled the more Mother fought her. Mother threatened her with witches and to this Marina responded, at the age of three, by dressing up as a witch and threatening Mother with a witch's broom.

When I was born I was a passive baby, and Mother must have been delighted at the change. When I imagine my infancy I would describe myself in the following way: She's a quiet, passive infant. She hardly ever cries but lies quietly in her crib, as if in a reverie. Her blind aunt Lucia claims that infants like Lilka seldom live beyond infancy – they're God's little angels, sent to earth for only a short while. And so, let her remain in her solipsistic reverie. No one wishes to interfere with her nature. No one brings her out with stimulating toys or games. They don't lift her just to play with her or to talk to her. It's convenient to have a quiet child, for a change. Once in a while her aunt bends over the crib and talks softly to the child. Her words bring out happy cooing sounds and the waving of tiny arms. The aunt, in her mind, claims this little angel as her own. If the child lives, she'll instil in her her own deep faith and religious fervour and teach her how to be saintly.

Ever since I could remember, there were bitter battles between Mother and Marina – battles that must have scared me into becoming even more undemanding and compliant. Moreover, ever since my birth a label had been stuck to me: I was nominated to be an angel – and the opposite label had stuck to Marina. Neither was accurate, and both were harmful to our development. In the camp we became somewhat independent of these labels, and we both felt that we had more in common with each other. But above all, a great deal of mutual empathy and friendship accompanied our relationship.

In Birkenau there was a *Kommando* called 'Kanada' – the name signified abundance and wealth. Only Jewish prisoners worked in it. They occupied a separate block, and there, after work, other prisoners crowded to purchase a pair of shoes, a sweater, or some underwear. Marina and I were also occasional clients in this unusual marketplace. Once we started receiving parcels from Warsaw, we were able to buy, for some garlic or onions, a pair of walking shoes or some socks and other daily necessities. The atmosphere at this market was friendly. It reminded me of the times when Mother would take me to a largely Jewish market in Warsaw. She loved bargaining and joking with the merchants. Sometimes she would be taken for being Jewish because she had black hair and eyes and spoke some Yiddish, which she had picked up in her childhood in eastern Poland.

The girls who worked in 'Kanada' endangered themselves daily by smuggling in, on their bodies, extra items of clothing that they 'organized' from the ramp – for that is where they worked, sorting out clothes left there by the newcomers. (In the camp vocabulary 'to organize' meant to obtain the necessary things without depriving or hurting another prisoner.) Some of them came from Warsaw, some from other European towns. The guards often searched these girls, and if they found anything they gave them a thrashing, but it didn't stop them from continuing their smuggling. We were grateful to them, for thanks to this marketplace we didn't have to wear those horrid wooden clogs we received as part of our camp uniforms, and if the camp authorities ordered us to give up our sweaters before the cold weather was over, we could buy sweaters from the girls in 'Kanada.'

In our *Kommando* there was a young secretary named Krysia. I spent many hours listening to her singing. She taught me words and arias from a number of operas. The one I'll never forget is an aria from *Die Tode Stadt* by Korngold. In this aria, lovers are separated by death. They sing of days of love, of death and of resurrection, when they'll be reun:ted. Each time I sang it, tears came to my eyes, for I thought of Jerzy. But Krysia also taught us a jaunty tune about a little jug. So, at the end of the working day, we used to sing this lively tune while we marched back to the camp.

One day we were nearing the camp, and the lively song ran ahead of us, right into the ears of SS-man Perschell, who, with arms akimbo and legs spread wide and dug firmly into the ground, greeted us with an ironic reproach for singing a happy tune in this place. To remind us where we were, he pointed to a pile of rocks by the road and ordered each of us to pick one up and jump a frog leap with it, right to the gate of the camp and all the way to our block. At first I was confused, trying to understand his order. By the time I understood it, all the lighter rocks were gone, and all that was left were heavy ones. He was screaming at us, and I realized that I didn't have any choice but to take one of the larger stones. I could hardly pick it up, let alone jump a frog leap with it. I stumbled but carried on, thinking that this was it – my last moment – for my heart was pounding as if it wanted to break into pieces. I was one of the last to cross the gate, but Perschell had gradually lost interest in this 'sport,' and once past the gate I let go of the rock. Shaking all over, I reached our block. So far, apart from being close to death during typhus, I was convinced that I had escaped death narrowly during this exercise. Marina was very sweet to me as she tucked me in, next to her, in our common bunk bed.

Next morning we woke up with terrible pain in our bodies, our hands trembling. We lined up for the roll-call. We dragged our feet all the way to our office block. Our *Kapo*, Halina, went to see Krug to complain to him about our last night's ordeal. We couldn't draw, our hands and arms still trembling. We never found out whether he interceded on our behalf, but we never had to jump a frog leap again. We continued singing on the way to the camp, only now we stopped quite a bit earlier, before our song could reach Perschell's ears.

My nineteenth birthday was on 9 July. The night before I spent a couple of hours writing a letter to Jerzy. I wrote about my love for him and about my hope for our prompt reunion – also about our duty to continue with our own development, with our studies, and with rebuilding our country. The next day a Polish male prisoner who worked in the gardens in Rajsko brought to the block where we worked some red roses and a letter from Jerzy: 'To me you are what a lighthouse is to a shipwrecked man, on the turbulent waters of the sea. You are the light guiding me safely to the shore.' After reading this and other profound expressions of his love I felt strengthened and imbued with a quiet hope that maybe, maybe ... I realized that I was also for him that important other who had helped him through these difficult times. When he was facing his own death, during the selection procedure, maybe it was me and my love that helped him through those difficult moments between life and death. I held onto the letter as long as I could, as it was a tangible reminder of the powerful emotional tie between us. Unfortunately, it got lost in the huge delousing we had to undergo soon after my birthday.

The great delousing took place on a Sunday in July. The day was somewhat cool but sunny. Waiting for our turn, we watched through the block window as the prisoners from the next block walked, naked, towards the sauna, carrying bundles of their clothing and throwing them into huge kettles, filled with liquid disinfectant, standing along the main road. When our turn came we deposited our bundles and went to the sauna, where we waited for our turn to shower. Next we were chased through cold showers by a *Kapo* armed with a wooden stick. After that, we were turned out into the field, between the blocks and the wires, where we spent hours looking for our clothes, which were spread out on the ground to dry in the bleak sun. Besides the SS-men, some male prisoners also supervised the delousing. As we walked around the field trying to locate our dresses we put on the white aprons that we found among the clothes. We were definitely embarrassed more by the presence of the male prisoners than by the presence of the SS-men, whom we didn't consider human.

During this delousing I lost the letter from Jerzy. I grieved this loss as if I had lost an arm. But its contents and its sentiment remain imprinted in my heart.

11
SOS

To facilitate the destruction of the Jews being transported to Auschwitz by trains from all parts of occupied Europe, the camp authorities extended the railway tracks to make the ramp, where selections took place, closer to the gas chambers and the crematoria.

Most of the transports used to arrive at night, and in the morning the air, thick with ashes, would let us know what had transpired during the night. I often wondered why the outside world was silent and did not react to these mass exterminations. After all, Jerzy and I had learned about these atrocities from the *Information Bulletin* issued by the Polish underground press a year before his arrest. We were so overwhelmed by these terrible reports. During my time in Auschwitz I thought that these acts of violence were known only in Poland and not known to the outside world. However, after the war I learned about the grim reality: the outside world was well informed about the atrocities committed on the Jews in Auschwitz and in the other camps. The Polish underground, from February 1940 onward, kept in daily contact through secret radio stations with the Polish government in exile, first in France and later in London, and informed the world about the Nazis' systematic destruction of European Jews.

By 1944 there existed in Poland close to one hundred military Home Army radio transmitters and about twelve radio stations under the aegis of the civilian Resistance. These stations regularly broadcast information about the fate of the Polish Jews – beginning with the resettlement of the Jews into the ghettos – and about the mass murders. As well, Polish emissaries conveyed information on microfilm to Polish diplomatic centres in the neutral countries of Europe. From there the information was passed on by diplomatic post to London.

One of the emissaries, Jan Karski, an eyewitness to the atrocities, played a historic role. In the late autumn of 1942 he sent from London an urgent SOS appealing to the whole world on behalf of Poland's Jews and Christians. When another emissary, Jan Nowak-Jezioranski, met with Karski in London, he found Karski frustrated and bitter. He claimed that his mission was not successful because everywhere he was met with disbelief, even from Jews. When Nowak-Jezioranski took over his mission, he also met with disbelief in all his contacts with parliamentarians, correspondents, and journalists. The Polish government in exile secured Karski a meeting with Prime Minister Winston Churchill, Anthony Eden, and three ministers from Britain's War Office. Karski informed them about the destruction of the European Jews. As well, he met with Dr Ignacy Schwarzbart, the representative of the Zionists. Before Schwarzbart introduced Karski to the Jewish representatives from the United States, he warned him not to mention the fact that at least two and a half million Jews had been exterminated by the Nazis because they would see it as a monstrous exaggeration, which Karski was spreading for his own, Polish reasons. What I hoped for was happening: the world was informed, but tragically the world did not respond.

However, even though the outside world remained indifferent to the fate of the European Jews, in Poland the Christian Poles were saving many Polish Jews through an organization called Zegota. Zegota grew out of the Polish underground Resistance, when it became clear that individual help for Jews was impossible without an extensive support network. At least two thousand Poles were put to death for helping Jews; thousands more were imprisoned, tortured, and sent to concentration camps; many thousands more took this risk, whether for days, for years, or for a moment. Emanuel Ringelbloom, the chronicler of the Warsaw Ghetto, recorded that Poles were shot just for throwing bread over the Ghetto wall. Poland was the only country in German occupied Europe where helping the Jews was punished with death – not only the ones who helped would be killed, but their whole families would also be destroyed.

Warnings about the automatic death penalty for those who tried to help Jews in occupied Poland were continually blared out on loudspeakers and posted in countless public places. The names and ages of those executed were also posted as a deterrent. Despite it all, the Jews were finding refuge among the Christian population, both in the cities and in the country villages.

One related incident comes to mind. It was a chilly autumn day in 1941 when Father came home in the evening, in the company of a stranger. The man was elderly, unshaven, and rather bedraggled-looking in his creased overcoat, carrying a paper bag in his hand. Father asked Mother to prepare a hot meal. Father took the stranger into his study and, pointing to the couch, asked if it would do for a few nights. The man gratefully accepted. After the meal, while the man was resting, Father told us about our guest. Father was passing by the Zacheta art gallery when he noticed, in the dusk, someone lying on the ground, covered with newspapers. Father woke him up, and it turned out that the man had escaped from the Ghetto and had nowhere to go. He also told Father that he was an artist. Father invited him to come and spend the night with us. To the rest of the household Father announced that the man was his old friend and would stay with us for a few days. Our visitor passed the time of day drawing, and for some hours he occupied himself by painting a watercolour portrait of Mother. Two or three days passed. Then Father arrived home one evening quite excited and happy. He had managed to find a more permanent place for our visitor in a small school for boys, run by the monks. He would be employed as an art teacher, and accommodation and meals would be provided in the monastery. We were overjoyed. The man, as a parting gift, offered Mother the watercolour portrait.

One Sunday a curfew was announced – the prisoners were not allowed out of their blocks. A big transport of Hungarian Jews was expected, and as the extended ramp was close to some of the blocks, we had to stay in. That's when I witnessed, with my own eyes, what has haunted my memory ever since.

> So many years
> so many springs and summers
> so many fallen leaves
> so much snow covered the earth
> so many mornings
> filled with larks' songs
> so many full moons
> and birthday celebrations
>
> But one memory
> one living image

in the dark crevices remains

Through the block's dirty window pane
I'm watching those
who sentenced
don't know their sentence

After the long trip
from some city of Europe
they line up obediently
They stand and wait
in the slow rain

They put down their suitcases
on the wet ground
They open up their umbrellas
The line moves slowly
Soon they'll take a warm shower
wash their tired bodies
after the long journey
Unpack their suitcases
and get ready
for the sweet nourishment of sleep
They believe
They want to believe
They were told so by those
who are trustworthy

All through July 1944 the war news continued to gladden our hearts. The Soviet front was moving rapidly westward, and on all other fronts the Allies made steady progress. On 28 July the Soviets took Brest-Litovsk, and on 31 July they were just thirteen kilometres from Warsaw.

Incredible news came on the first of August. This date marked the beginning of one of the most bloody revolts of the war – the Warsaw Uprising. I was quite shaken, for this was the moment for which we were preparing during the years of occupation, and it was happening without my participation as a nurse. I was thinking of all my friends taking arms, helping with communications and with first aid. Warsaw, the first occupied city in all of Europe, was attempting to free itself of the enemy.

I waited anxiously for further news. On 1 August the Polish flag was placed on the tallest building in Warsaw and in Poland, the Prudential. On 18 August the Zoska battalion of the Home Army liberated the Jewish camp in Gesiowka, where Jews of many European countries were imprisoned. But the news coming through the radio in SS-man Krug's office was not very cheerful. The uprising continued for sixty-two days, until 2 October. The Polish Army of the Resistance wanted to participate in freeing Warsaw from German occupation. The moment seemed appropriate: the Soviet army was on the other side of the Vistula River. Surely it would join in the liberation of Warsaw. But how wrong the Poles were in thinking of the Soviet Union as their ally. The Soviet troops stood there, watching the city being destroyed, thousands of its citizens slaughtered, thousands taken into captivity by the Germans. All in all, 250,000 citizens, including civilians, perished. At the end, all the surviving citizens of Warsaw were ordered out of the city. The Germans then continued dynamiting the remaining buildings until 85 per cent of the city was destroyed. What a terrible ending for the thousands of Polish insurgents – and for Warsaw, barely rebuilt after the 1939 bombings. Warsaw, the proud capital of Poland, lay in ruins.

The Swedish writer Ture Nerman wrote: 'The battle of Warsaw is the most heroic of all the battles carried out in history by humankind. Warsaw gained forever an honourable place in history. Warsaw will become a holy city.' The BBC, after the defeat of Warsaw, sent this message to all the countries of Europe: 'Warsaw insurgents have achieved a task unsurpassed even by the regular armies of the Great Allies in this war.'

Soon the camp started to fill up with insurgents from the uprising. For most of them it was just a stopover before they were sent to a prisoner-of-war camp in Oberlangen. In talking with the young insurgents, I met some who gave me news of my friend Joanna Berland. She was wounded at the beginning of the uprising and removed to a field hospital. They also told me that, after I was arrested, her parents were sent to Majdanek, where they were killed by the Nazis. It was only after the war that Joanna told me the details. The morning after our arrest she had gone to notify the other members of our group about my detention. This was part of the routine after someone was arrested. She returned home just before the curfew. The apartment was sealed – her parents had been taken to Majdanek. What an incredible stroke of fate. Had my arrest not taken place, Joanna too would have been arrested along with her parents. It turned out that their maid had betrayed them – as a reward, she received their apartment. Mrs Dlugoszowska, a widow and a mother of two sons who were our friends, took Joanna into her home, where she'd stayed until the end of the war. Both Dlugoszowski brothers were killed in the uprising.

In September and October the camp authorities started to organize the evacuation of the Polish male prisoners. As the eastern front was moving west, the Germans wished to move the men into Germany, where they would be further exploited in the service of the Third Reich. At the end of September a message came from Jerzy that his transport would be leaving the following Sunday, from a ramp close to our part of the camp. Where were they going to send him? What would become of him? Would I ever see him again?

With these questions on my mind, I went with Marina to see him off. The ramp, after its extension, could be seen from our part of the camp. Soon we spotted his tall, slightly stooping silhouette. He saw us too. He waved, and with a wide sweep of his arm he threw a small stone in our direction. The stone was wrapped with a piece of paper, held by a rubber band. On the paper – a message: 'Dear Girls, see you after the Liberation, Your Jerzy.'

Soon the same fate met Father, Tytus, Wojtek Kubasiewicz, and most of the male political prisoners. The difference was that they were travelling together. They had wanted to take Jerzy out of his transport by substituting another prisoner, but he wouldn't agree to that. He felt that it was his destiny to go with his transport. Was he a fatalist? No. After the war I found out that Jerzy was evacuated together with the hospital staff: doctors and other male nurses. He worked with them, and he wished to go with them.

It was hard to find out where the transports were going. Buchenwald was the place most frequently mentioned. As the Soviet troops were marching through Poland, the Germans were trying to remove the able-bodied men before the Soviets entered Auschwitz. They sent them to various workstations around Buchenwald.

As a result of the evacuation of the men, Marina and I were transferred, sometime in early January 1945, to the building office in Auschwitz I, where my father and brother had worked before their departure. We hated this idea, as it meant that we would have to separate from our companions, Genia, Halina, Krysia, Vera, and others. But we were helpless against this order, and we were marched, by a guard, to Auschwitz I and led to a brick building where our future sleeping quarters were located. The room was not overcrowded, and we settled down, each of us on a middle bunk of the triple bunk beds. For the first time in months we were to sleep alone, not having to share the bed with each other. When the prisoners came from their work, we found out who shared the triple bunk beds with us. Above me was a German prostitute, below me, a German Jehovah's Witness. Marina was in similar company.

In the morning we were led to our new workplace, the building office. A friendly Silesian Volksdeutch prisoner was our guide. He informed us that he knew our father and brother when they had worked there. Inside the office we met the chief architect, an elderly Hungarian Jew, who greeted us warmly and showed us the drafting tables where our father and brother had worked. We felt warmly welcomed to this new place and gradually acquainted ourselves with the rest of the staff.

One incident from those days remains in my memory. One day Marina and I were told to prepare for an outing to a location outside the camp to take measurements of some buildings. This type of activity was quite familiar to us, as we used to go out on similar assignments from our Birkenau office. Our Czech friends used to chuckle each time we were sent on '*pomiary*,' which in Polish meant to take measurements, but in Czech meant something close to a lovers' meeting.

We set out with the working drawings towards the gate thinking that a *Posten* would be waiting to escort us. But there was no guard, no *Aufseherin*. We showed our working drawings to the SS-man and explained our mission. To our immense surprise he let us go, on our own. We followed our map, and after a while we reached the old, dilapidated house that we were to measure. When we went down to measure the cellar, we found some half-rotten potatoes. We selected the most healthy-looking ones and tucked them into the bosom space above our belts, delighted, as the parcels had stopped coming from Warsaw at the beginning of the Warsaw Uprising and nagging hunger was again our constant companion.

As we walked back to the camp, we were happy and elated. We felt free, and we even considered a dash for freedom. But the sad reality was that we were wearing our prison dresses, had nowhere to go, and the towers with guards all around the camp made escape very hazardous. This adventure reminded us of an escapade from our childhood

days, in Milosna, when Marina was eight and I was six. For a long time
we had been fascinated by a distant and mysterious windmill, waving
its huge wings on the horizon. We had spun stories about it, and the
more we fantasized about it the more anxious we became to see it at
close quarters, to discover its mysteries, to find out what kind of a
magician or witch lived in it. One bright summer day we set out on our
adventure, without revealing to anyone our destination, knowing that
we would be met with many objections.

Marina, an eight-year-old Don Quixote,
I, her little Sancho Panza,
set out one sunny day
to touch with our eyes,
to feel on our cheeks
mighty waves of air
stirred by the wings.

Across the meadows,
through seas of cornflowers,
flames of poppies, scattering of daisies.
Across the fields,
divided by murky ditches,
with flurries of bees and butterflies
and a startled bird
who made her nest in tall grasses.
Lark's song
trembled in the summer air,
wafted down from the blue,
accompanying us
across dark marshes,
glimmering brooks where
a sudden splash of water
announced a frog
surprised by our chatty presence.

The windmill grew, numinous,
filling up with our adventure,
charged with ineffable mystery.
Huge, holy, coveted the sky.
A winged cathedral.

A sudden anguished feeling.
The dying sun throws long shadows.
We should be going back –
they'll worry at home.

We returned to the camp. At the gate they asked us about the *Posten*.
'We didn't get one,' we replied to an astounded SS-man.

Part III

From Winter to Spring (January–April 1945)

12
Walking to Breslau

My memories at this point dissolve, and I can't remember much except that soon we heard the women prisoners were going to be evacuated from Auschwitz I. The departure would take place on foot, as the Allies had bombed the railway tracks to the nearest railway station, Breslau. The Silesian prisoner promised to 'organize' some better walking shoes for us. He'd been very kind to us, once in a while bringing us some extra food.

Every day we heard the airplanes bombing nearby towns, and we realized that we were going to leave this place just days or hours before the Soviet troops liberated it.

Before the Silesian prisoner managed to get us some better walking shoes, we were told that the next day we would have to leave. My memory of the events that followed is both vivid and vague. Vivid is the emotional climate – a sense of relief about the change, about being able to leave this accursed place, where we had spent almost two years – two painful, frightened, and hungry years. Vague are the details of geography, of people. What I do remember is that we received no extra clothing to wear for this march, even though it was the end of January, but we did get two loaves of bread each and some lumps of sugar. This was to sustain our already-emaciated bodies for three days. We were allowed to take other items such as sheets or blankets, and Marina and I decided to take one sheet each – the thought of having a piece of clean cloth to put our heads on, wherever we would be spending our nights, was very comforting – and we carried the sheets even though, after several hours of marching, we gradually parted with most of our bread – it turned out to be too heavy to carry. We did, however, hang onto our lumps of sugar, which we rationed out, carefully, every few hours.

How much energy a lump of sugar could provide to a body that was too weak to carry a loaf of bread!

Whenever I now drive in the Caledon area, near Toronto, along a country road that winds up and down so that its ribbon clearly unfolds ahead of me, I see in my mind's eye a strange procession: columns and columns of women, in prison dresses and jackets, white kerchiefs covering their heads. Some are carrying bundles in their hands, some bending under the weight of heavy loads on their backs.

There were some young country girls among us, sent to Auschwitz for running away from labour farms or camps, and they had grabbed whatever they could carry and were obstructing the road with their heavy bundles. Whenever I bumped into one of them I had trouble regaining my balance, and I marvelled at their strength. It was to them that we gave our bread, as they seemed to have Herculean powers to carry anything.

After we left the camp we stayed on the road. There were farm fields on both sides covered with snow and sometimes a small community, with several single-family houses clustered around a small country church. We must have passed by some larger towns, such as Opole, Katowice, or Sosnowiec, which were on a more direct route to Breslau. But those towns were being bombed, and we were led along the roads that were clear of bombings.

With every kilometre I could feel energy leaving my body, blisters on the heels of my feet getting more and more painful, my lips becoming parched, as the thirst was becoming harder to bear than hunger. Marina shared the same fate but kept comforting me.

The worst time was when we had to stop because the road would narrow down while cutting through a small village. My stiffened muscles would relax, temporarily, as I squatted on the road together with hundreds of my companions, waiting for others to catch up. To rise from my squat was almost impossible. It was Marina who helped me get up, who comforted me with the promise of a good night's rest.

That first night the long column broke up, and we turned towards the dark shape of a huge barn standing in a field by the road. Its enormous doors were wide open, and as we entered, Marina quickly scanned the situation and pushed me gently in the direction of a ladder that led to the second floor, where the hay was stored. The clay floor all around us was already covered with a human carpet. Prisoners had dropped down as soon as they entered the barn. Marina and I climbed the ladder and, on the hay, lined our soft nests with our clean sheets. We sucked the nourishing sweetness of the sugar cubes as we slid shoes wet with snow off our aching feet. Soon the great silence of uneasy sleep, of tortured dreams, filled the barn. Marina and I whispered to each other and planned to consider hiding in the hay in the morning – maybe no one would miss us.

Heavy sleep that followed was gradually restoring our bodies for the next day's trials. However, tired as I was, I was awakened by a nagging pressure in my bladder and moved away from our place to relieve the pressure. Inside the barn it was pitch dark. The air was warmed by the heat of hundreds of bodies and filled with heavy breathing, loud sighs, and occasionally a frightened cry from one of the sleep-drunk travellers covering the vast clay floor.

I was groping in the dark, trying to find my way back to where Marina was sleeping, when suddenly I felt the hay under my feet sliding me down into the darkness below. I was falling, grabbing and trying to hold onto a bundle of hay, falling onto a breathing, live mass of human bodies, lost in their dark dreams. A tower of Babel erupted and I heard around me a multitude of languages calling out in sleep-shrouded voices. I felt myself being shrugged off, passed on by invisible hands, from body to body, while I kept calling softly: 'Marina, Marina, I fell down, where are you?'

Momentarily, a sudden flash of memory came to me about a story that my mother used to tell. She and Father, together with another couple, Stenia and Henryk Plucinski, set out one year to pay homage to the Black Madonna at Jasna Gora in Czestochowa. As they neared the monastery they suddenly found themselves lifted and carried towards the icon by the crowd, a pilgrimage of half-crazed women, who were rushing, on their knees, towards the shrine. Mother lost her balance and was carried away from my father and her friends. When she finally regained her balance she was inside the church, kneeling and praying with great reverence, her face buried in her hands. When she uncovered her face, she saw that all the time she'd been facing the back of the church, her back towards the Black Madonna. She looked around and saw her friend Stenia in the same position. When they saw each other they burst into hysterical giggles.

This memory cheered me up in the dark barn, and I was hopeful that I would locate Marina. To show me where she was, she lit a match! The German guard lit a flashlight and threatened to shoot. One match –

enough to point the way, but also enough to set the whole bloody barn on fire! Remorseful, I slowly climbed my way in her direction and collapsed on my white island into heavy sleep.

In the darkness of the January dawn we were awakened by the loud 'Raus, Raus' of the guards as they shoved the prisoners out into the cold, wintry air. Marina and I were terrified, as we couldn't put our stiff and wet shoes on our blistered and swollen feet. Finally we managed to limp down. The previous night's plans to hide in the hay dissolved when we heard shots being fired at those who tried to linger. Later we learned that after everyone had left the German shepherd dogs were let loose to sniff out any reluctant bodies.

The pain of our swollen and blistered feet, squeezed into our wet, tight shoes, competed with hunger pains sucking at our stomachs as we moved along the road. The darkness of the early winter morning was occasionally sprinkled by a shaded light in the windows of the country homesteads we were passing as the occupants began their morning chores. Farm dogs started their early greetings, and gradually dim, wintery light brightened the horizon.

Marina and I talked to the other prisoners, and we learned that some girls who were trying to hide in the hay were found by the dogs and were shot on the spot. Our sugar put some new strength into our bodies, but soon it wore out and I started daydreaming as I tried to keep up with the column. My dreams went to Jerzy, and I wondered if this march would bring me closer to him. I had no idea where they'd transported him the previous autumn. Was it to Buchenwald?

Our column stopped on the main street of a village. I was shaken out of my daydream. How much longer? I felt so weak – I couldn't imagine going on. To keep my mind active, I tried to pray, but my thoughts wandered and I couldn't recall any prayers. I begged Marina to let me stop here. Maybe they'd leave me behind and some farmers would take me in later. But she was firm. She would never leave me behind. I gathered my strength and kept moving.

But we were slipping behind, and we dropped back closer and closer to the tail end of the column. Marina was also warming up to the idea of lingering and maybe being left behind by the guards. We sobered up when we heard the gunshots, behind us, at the rear of the column. Yes, they were shooting the malingerers like dogs.

We saw the white fields around us, the grey skies above, and ahead of us that long, broad snake of a column. We were also aware of the constant rumbling in the air, of airplanes passing above us and, on the horizon, flashes of explosions lighting up the skies. We were so close to freedom, and yet moving away from it with every slow, painful step. Even now Soviet forces might be liberating Auschwitz. How senseless this war was – a dark force that pushed us on towards another, unknown destiny. Somewhere, to the west, there was Jerzy, there was Father, and there was Tytus. And our youngest sister, Zosia. We didn't know what had happened to her after she was separated from us and put in a quarantine block, then transported out. Where? That was over a year and a half ago, in May 1943. Just before Mother died.

Towards the evening my exhaustion reached its peak – we stumbled through a village. Because the road narrowed, there was a bottleneck, and we had to wait. We squatted down to rest. I was in a daze. My body was so weak, life's force was gradually draining away.

The lumps of sugar helped and didn't help – they gave an illusion of help, momentarily. I didn't think of death, however – death was an intellectual concept, and my mind couldn't deal with it. All I knew was that I wanted to stop, to curl up, and to sleep. I still tried to think of good things, of hopeful things, of Jerzy waiting for me somewhere in a camp in Germany, loving me, needing me, of our future together. I evoked the past, I evoked my safe and happy childhood, as I moved along as in a dream.

> Tall years, take me.
> Lead me in
> and out of months, weeks and days
> of my childhood, my youth.
>
> Where is that little girl?
> Bare toes dance over rain-washed Aprils,
> May-time Marys sadly gaze
> from their icons.
> Where are you dandelion gold,
> sunflower round faces – my gifts for Mary?
> 'Mother of Jesus,
> pray for me now
> and in the hour of my death,'
> lips whisper, eyes gaze with blue reverence
> at the dark sorrow.
> 'Forget-me-nots
> are fairy-tale flowers'

Sing me a song.
Carry me Auntie, my feet are sore.
Don't step there,
a stone will trip you.

Why are you blind?
Don't die.
Your black skirts smell of tobacco
when I bury my tears in them.
Tell me another story
and love me always.

Manger hay is scented with dreams.
Melodies of ancient carols
sing in the hay's dry blades:
'Lullaby my little Jesus
my little pearl.
lullaby my little Jesus
my little pet.'

Where are you, short-skirted summers,
first school days in pigtail pride?
I can read!
I'll read to you
the fairy tales you forgot.
I'll read to you a bedtime story
and tuck you in your lonely bed.
Never again will I spill tobacco
in your old wooden trunk.

But these thoughts and memories slowly eluded me and my mind went blank. To stop from fainting, from losing consciousness, I tried to repeat lines of well-known poems, but my mind was losing the words. I searched for a prayer and repeated Hail Marys, but these so-familiar words also slipped away. I whispered to Marina: 'Leave me here, I can't go on, I'll stay behind, they'll let me be.'

Again, she was firm and helped me gently up as the column started moving slowly. 'Do you hear those shots? They're shooting the weak ones that can't go on – they would shoot us, too.' We moved slowly on, every step an unbelievable effort. But soon it got dark, and there was a prospect of another night's sweet rest. There was the shape of another barn in a snow-covered field, and the column broke as the women started entering the dark interior.

As soon as we entered we were enveloped by the sweet smell of animal bodies and of cow manure. Oh, this couldn't be true! We were hosted by gentle, white and brown cows with their calves. Some women knew how to milk the cows, and soon they handed out cupfuls of fresh milk. We hadn't tasted milk for almost two years. It was warm and sweet. And the smell of cow manure held such nostalgia for me – childhood memories of our summers at Aunt Josephine's farm, in the eastern territories. This smell meant safety. This taste meant freedom.

Marina and I spread our now not-so-white sheets on the sweet, dung-smelling straw, next to the warm body of a mother cow. The beast seemed indifferent and she let us be. Her calf was on her other side. Soon we fell into the sleep of babies, full of life-giving milk, shared with us by these large, mute, innocent companions of our fate.

The next morning, refreshed by deep sleep, we got up to the sounds of guards shouting. We emerged from the barn and scanned the countryside. The skies were grey, and the white cover of snow on the fields around us made me wonder how many more hours, how many more kilometres, we were away from our destiny.

The previous night's milk gave us some energy and some hope. We joined the column on the road and resumed our journey. Our blistered feet ached, and the cold January wind made us shiver, but we continued on this senseless march while the 'caw, caw' of the crows followed us together with the occasional barking of village dogs and the hopeful rumble of the planes above.

I don't recall how far we walked, but I do remember nearing a railway station. Some women recognized it as Breslau. There was a cattle train waiting for us. Ah, the luxury of train travel! We embarked, not knowing our destination. We sat on the bare floor of the car, and soon a half-sleep, half-daze enveloped me as I slid into a trance of fragmented memories, fragmented dreams.

I was shaken out of this strange state by the noise of the doors being opened and by the commotion among the women in the car. Marina told me that we had to get out to empty our bladders. We jumped down on the ramp – we were surrounded by a dark forest. The guards stood along the ramp, their rifles at the ready. They shouted the familiar '*Schnell, Schnell*' as we hitched up our dresses and squatted on the gravel. I didn't feel any sense of shame or humiliation. In my mind any feeling of shame was chased away by my deep contempt for the men who watched us – let them feel shame, let them turn their eyes away. Some did. We scrambled back into the cars. Once again, we were on our way.

We arrived in the evening. The train stopped, and we wondered where we were. As we tumbled out of the cattle car there was confusion, darkness, shouts. My body slowly and painfully unfolded from the twisted position in which I spent the night. My muscles were sore, and my feet hurt. I felt terribly thirsty, as we'd had nothing to drink since the milk in the barn the night before.

The word 'Ravensbruck' was repeated over and over. We knew that it was a women's camp, but we didn't see any blocks or buildings. In front of us loomed the huge, dark shape of a tent. Enormous. We were pushed inside the opening, as if it were a huge mouth swallowing us. Near the entrance we noticed a free spot on the clay floor. We flopped down. By now we were reduced to this one animal need: to curl up and sleep. But a woman urged us on, pointing to the dim inside of the tent. We recognized the familiar shape of the triple bunk beds. Beds! We moved along and accommodated ourselves on the middle bunk. The bed shook as above us two husky Ukrainian girls laughed and talked in loud voices. Soon we didn't hear anything, for we drifted into a deep and heavy sleep, with the old, white sheets under our heads.

In the middle of the night, a strange commotion above our heads and the delicious smell of soup woke us up. It turned out that while we were sleeping, the Ukrainian women prisoners had raided the camp kitchen and had stolen kettles of soup. One such kettle was above our heads, on the top bunk, and the two women were ladling out bowls full of soup to everyone. As we were feasting on the delicious soup, gratitude, laughter, and fears of retaliation blended with the sweet taste of turnips.

After this unexpected treat from our Ukrainian companions, Marina and I ventured out into the misty and chilly January morning to see where we were. Many prisoners were already out, standing on the side of a wide road. Across, on the other side, a huge crowd of Ravensbruck prisoners had gathered to check if they could find a friend, a sister, or a mother among the miserable fiends from Auschwitz.

As we milled around, we heard our names being shouted by someone on the other side. The voice came from a tall girl whose face looked familiar. Zosia. Our first impulse was to run to her, and we burst out onto the road, but a fearsome German *Kapo* was on our backs with her wooden club. So we moved back, into the contaminated ranks of the Auschwitz prisoners, and started our discourse above the voices of other prisoners.

We asked Zosia where she had spent the previous year. She replied that she had passed most of it in Pawiak in Warsaw, and then, before the uprising, she had been sent here. Zosia's first question was about Mother. We told her that she'd died of pneumonia, soon after Zosia left. There was silence on the other side, and then, with a choking voice, she replied that she had guessed so, because no one else mentioned Mother in the letters to her in prison. We stopped this exchange of news because the three of us were crying. Only she cried alone, on the other side of the road. Then another, tear-strangled query – she asked about Father and Tytus. We replied that we didn't know about their destination, because they had been evacuated to Germany, maybe to Buchenwald or Dachau. She shouted that she had to leave for her work unit – in a sewing *Kommando* – Wanda Wilczanska and Professor Bujalska were there too. Professor Bujalska had been my literature teacher in high school, and Wanda Wilczanska I had met in Pawiak, soon after our arrest.

We were amazed at Zosia's height. When she left us she was still a little girl of fourteen. During the year in prison she grew to be the tallest one in the whole family. Later she told us that she also had been confused. She was looking for her two tall sisters – as she always remembered us – and here were these two short girls with her sisters' faces and voices.

I could never recall much of that first day in Ravensbruck. After Zosia left, we probably went back to our bunk bed and speculated on what would happen to us next. It was obvious that we weren't going to stay here; hence the temporary accommodation in the huge tent. We were still exhausted from our three-day march and must have slept most of that day.

The next thing I remember was a miracle: I woke up in a white bed, wearing a rough but clean nightgown – the room looked and smelled like the camp hospital. Marina was on the bed next to me, also wearing a clean nightgown and smiling mysteriously at me. She explained what had happened. After our meeting in front of the tent, Zosia went to her German *Kapo* in the sewing *Kommando* to ask if her two sisters, who were in the Auschwitz transport, could stay in Ravensbruck and work with her in the sewing group. As I found out later, it was a heroic step on Zosia's part, as the woman was very strict and the prisoners from Auschwitz had the terrible reputation of being filthy and crawling with lice infected with typhus. Professor Bujalska later told us that Zosia walked into the office of the *Kapo* proudly, with a royal gait.

Thus we were transported from the tent to the hospital, where we were deloused, scrubbed, and put in clean beds. One strange thing about the whole event is that I don't remember any of it – neither being transported to the hospital, nor being bathed and deloused. A total amnesia descended, as if these things had never happened. After a couple of days of nourishing food and rest in the hospital, we were ready to join the sewing *Kommando*.

But here too I'm not able to recall the events – being there ... working ... the other people. I know that Professor Bujalska was there and my two sisters and Wanda Wilczanska. Otherwise, those few weeks are a blank – most probably from the total exhaustion that I suffered on that three-day march.

13
Bergen-Belsen

Our career in Ravensbruck ended after a few weeks. One day, early in March, we were told to prepare for another transport. There was nothing to pack – we'd been travelling light in the last two years. Hundreds of young women prisoners lined up on the ramp. We were embarking on another cattle train, but this time Zosia, Marina, and I were together.

This journey is again a blank. But I recall vividly getting off the train as it stopped by a beautiful, ancient forest. There was a road, lightly covered with snow, running through it, and as we walked along this road our hearts sang. We had not been out in nature for such a long time, and this forest seemed enchanting. Tall elms, huge chestnut trees, mixed with graceful pines, resplendent spruces. The air, filled with an early spring chorus of birds, reminded us that there still was life and beauty in this world. We felt optimistic, hopeful – nothing bad could happen to us in this beautiful forest. The weather was typical for early March: at one moment the sun flooded the forest, and then, a few moments later, a dark cloud would send thick, heavy snowflakes into our faces.

None of us knew where we were or where we were heading. After some time, we saw ahead of us the gate to another camp. We didn't know its name, but as we walked through the gate we noticed a woman prisoner whom we remembered from Birkenau. She was a *Lagerälteste*, and here she seemed to hold the same position.

Stenia Starostka also recognized Marina and me. The sight of this woman didn't cheer us up. She was well known for her cruelty, especially towards 'musulmans' – prisoners who, divested of all strength, of all the aggression necessary for living, were not able even to move. She would kick them with contempt and hatred. Did she do so because, on some level, she was aware that their projected aggression had to be contained by aggressors like herself? She was tolerant only of those prisoners who were healthy and able to work. As we, workers from the *Bauburo*, had always looked clean and neat, she had treated us well. Now she remembered our faces – Marina and I had always been in the first row of our small column.

As we walked towards some blocks, we heard the name of our new home: Bergen-Belsen. The name meant nothing to us. It was only later that we found out that this was another death camp. We also realized that this was where the prisoners from the big tent in Ravensbruck must have been sent, while we were moved to the sewing *Kommando*.

We were led to an empty block. I mean empty – no bunk beds, no benches, no mattresses. Empty of furnishings, and full of women with hardly room enough to sit down, to stretch, to lie down.

Some prisoners brought a large container of thin turnip soup. We were given metal bowls and spoons. Even though the soup was thin and watery, drinking some warm liquid felt good. It soon got dark, and the three of us curled up on the bare floor and went to sleep.

In the morning we got up, stretched our stiff limbs, and went to line up outside for some warm herbal tea that was being ladled out by the women who worked in the kitchen. We talked to our companions and learned that only those prisoners here who worked received food – food, meaning some turnips. There was no bread in Germany; there was none in Bergen-Belsen.

Inside the block I looked out through a dirty window pane. I saw a yard, with several blocks surrounding it. In the middle of the yard a large mound, almost a small hill, was covered with a thick layer of snow. Old and wasted-looking male prisoners walked slowly and shakily around the mound. They looked like the shades from Dante's Inferno. Some of them stopped to rest, in a frozen stupor, on the side of the snow-covered mound – this sight was most distressing and depressing.

In a day or two there was a thaw, and the snow started to melt. A terrible truth was revealed to all: the mound was made of frozen human corpses.

This place was deadly – a place to perish, to die of hunger, sickness, and exhaustion. Once a day some watery turnip soup was dished out for us. We felt weaker with every hour.

But soon a messenger came from camp headquarters and asked for one of the sisters who used to work in the *Bauburo* in Auschwitz. Marina stepped forward. She was told that she was going to work in a *Kommando* that made signs for the camp. She replied that she would gladly do so as long as her two sisters could join her. To our joy, we were allowed to do so. This move meant hope.

We were led to a block for prisoners who were employed in some capacity or other, and so there was hope that Zosia and I would also receive jobs. For the time being we were happy to nourish ourselves on some bits of food that Marina saved for us. And, of course, we now slept on bunk beds.

Another messenger showed up a few days later and asked for the other sister who had worked in the *Bauburo* in Auschwitz. Our fame was spreading! It must have been the hateful Stenia who remembered us. I was happy, but also a little scared. How would I manage without Marina, who was always on hand in the Auschwitz office to explain my work to me.

The next morning I was led by a messenger to my new place of work. The block where the office was located was not far away. I entered a large room with several drafting tables. There were only two workers here. An elderly Czech Jew was the chief architect. A young Jewish girl from Poland was the secretary. I introduced myself and explained that I used to work in a *Bauburo* in Auschwitz. The man, whose name was Adam, told me that there wasn't much work here. The girl's name was Ala. They explained that the rest of the staff had died of typhus.

This office – a parody – would have been funny had it not been so tragic. Once in a while an SS-man appeared to give the architect some instructions. Even though the office couldn't have been very efficient it seemed that the SS-man wanted to keep it going as long as possible. After all, the Germans were playing one big game of make-believe. As long as the SS-man could prove his usefulness in the camp, he wouldn't have to fear being sent to the front. And the front seemed just days away.

The best thing about working in this office was our daily trip to the SS kitchen for a container of hot, thick soup, which I took to my block to share with my sisters.

One day I went to work, and no one was in the office. I carried on, but at the end of the day I was told that the office would have to close because my two co-workers had contracted typhus. This was the end of my career as an architectural draftsman in Bergen-Belsen.

So once again Zosia and I were unemployed and hungry. Days dragged by as we waited, hoping that something would turn up for us. Then one day we heard that the authorities needed help in the camp kitchen. Eagerly we applied and were accepted.

That first morning we set out in the dark, as the work started at five. Again, I don't recall much, except that we had to carry, all through the day, some very heavy kettles. At the end of this seemingly endless day, exhausted and shaky, we sat to our meal: a bowl of thick, hot soup. To our incredible disappointment, the sight and smell of it, which usually would have delighted us, made us sick to our stomachs. Dejected, we decided that this job was not for us – or we were not made for it. We went to our block and collapsed for the night.

Marina came back from work one day excited and happy – she brought from her *Kommando* a can of peaches in thick, sweet syrup. Some girls had found a hiding place in which the SS-men were storing all sorts of provisions, mainly canned goods. So, from then on, the girls were distributing the cans to all the prisoners in their *Kommando*. It was a secret and dangerous activity.

We managed to open that first can and treated ourselves to this delicacy. The sweet syrup felt heavenly on our tongues, the soft fruit melted in our mouths. But the effects were disastrous. A couple of hours later we were sitting in the outdoor latrines, located in the field between the blocks and the wires. The night was starry and bright. On the horizon the skies exploded, for the front was just kilometres away. Our stomachs competed with the explosions at the front line. But we were so happy. The end was near, and if these sweet preserves didn't kill us, we would soon be celebratating our liberation.

Many SS guards were disappearing into the surrounding forest. Those who continued working in the camp started wearing a white band on their arm – a symbol of surrender. Many prisoners were disappearing into the hospital, as the typhus epidemic was raging in the camp. Marina and I were happy that we'd already had typhus, but we worried about Zosia, who could catch it at any time.

The Germans were short of help in the block, and I was told to serve as a helper. My job was to sweep the block and keep it neat – and to achieve this I would have to yell at the malingerers. I knew that I wouldn't be able to do that and would lose this despicable job. Miracu-

lously, I was delivered from this dilemma by a sudden attack of laryn-
gitis – only a whisper would come out of my mouth. Mercifully, with
my voice gone, I also lost my job.

In those last days before liberation, I had one more job: sorting out
some civilian clothes, probably from the last transports that arrived in
the camp. At that time Zosia started to run a high fever. We didn't
want her to go to the hospital, as she would surely catch typhus or
other diseases there. So I hid her under a pile of clothes and hoped for
the best.

Part IV

The Taste of Freedom (April 1945–June 1946)

14

My Egg of Resurrection

That cool but sunny April morning, as I was busy working, I suddenly heard a strange noise coming from the main camp road. It grew into a loud roar. I left my pile of clothes, threw on my prison jacket, and rushed to the door. I stepped outside, and with my bewildered eyes I saw a tank rumbling along the road. There were some soldiers on top of the tank, and I thought they were black Americans, as their faces were shining black. Later I realized that the black on their faces was camouflage so that their faces wouldn't shine in the night. The soldiers were British.

In front of this tank there was a jeep. It stopped not far away from me. The driver jumped down and ran towards me. All I saw were his eyes, gazing intently at me, and the three stripes on his battledress sleeve. What did he see? A drawn face, with pronounced cheekbones, sunken cheeks, and a pair of huge blue eyes, now full of tears. By then I didn't see anything else – the tears were rolling down my face, covering my vision. Tears of sorrow and tears of joy. Sorrow for those who didn't make it – tears of joy for being reborn on this wonderful day in April. The soldier turned around abruptly and ran back to his jeep, as if remembering something. He took this something out of his jeep, ran back towards me, and put it into the pocket of my prison jacket. I was stunned but also embarrassed by a crowd of women suddenly milling behind me, with outstretched hands, begging the man for cigarettes. I was living through an almost-religious moment. The dark shade of Thanatos was receding, giving room to Eros, the god of life. I felt an immense gratitude to this unknown British soldier who gave me the gift of Life and Freedom together with this mysterious something that felt like a small can and an egg. My Egg of Resurrection.

I looked at the egg and the small can of strawberry preserve. The soldier must have kept these nourishing items in his jeep as his emergency ration.

Then I remembered my sisters and ran into the block to look for them. Zosia had miraculously lost her fever and was now talking animatedly with Marina and some other girls who were gathering by the door. I showed them my gifts. Later on, when the first joy and excitement wore off, I found a bowl and a fork. I broke the egg into the bowl and beat it until it was stiff and frothy. I added the jam and beat it into a delicious pink dessert. We found some spoons and celebrated our liberation, praising the unknown British soldier, praising the entire British army for delivering us from evil on this memorable day in April. Later on I learned it was 15 April 1945. There were no calendars in the camp.

On the fiftieth anniversary of the end of the Second World War, Canadian television showed a documentary depicting Bergen-Belsen and the fate of the camp after the liberation. The film stated that a British detachment in the north of Germany had stumbled on the hidden Belsen concentration camp near Hanover, to find typhus raging, forty thousand prisoners sick, starving, and dying, and thirteen thousand corpses stacked on the ground – there was no crematorium in Belsen. The SS guards, now reduced to the status of workers, were helping to clean up the camp. Their task was to carry the corpses to the three huge graves that they were forced to dig. Both men and women were shown carrying these half-decayed bodies – their limbs dangling, their heads hanging back, the emaciated carcasses displaying protruding bones. Even though I spent several weeks in this godforsaken place, I had no idea of the totality of horror that transpired in this death camp, for while I was a prisoner my vision was limited to the small area in which I lived and worked, even though my awareness grew broader as I heard of many people dying in the hospital. As well, I did witness, at the very beginning of my stay, the mound of frozen corpses in the yard between the blocks.

Soon after the British arrived the German commander of the camp, Kramer, took the British commander on a tour. The British army jeep was driven all around the camp: on one sidestep stood Kramer, on the other the British commander. This sight evoked a variety of profound feelings in me – most important, a sense of gratification that our hope triumphed at the end, that we were not forgotten and abandoned by the world.

Of course, I also wondered how Kramer felt as the full scope of his criminality was being gradually revealed to the bewildered eyes of the British commander. Was he excusing himself with the usual: 'I was only following orders'? Or was he proudly telling him that he was a decent chap because, instead of giving out to the still-healthy prisoners the poisoned bread that was stored in a special block, he decided to save them and to surrender the camp? Was there such a block with poisoned bread? This item of news circulated among the prisoners, but I never found out whether it was fact or fiction.

After the liberation we were moved to the nearby town of Zelle. We received accommodation in buildings previously occupied by the SS guards who ran the camp. These small apartment blocks had spartan furnishings. I was elated at the cleanliness of the place, the hot baths, clean dishes, and the freedom to make decisions. Together with Marina, I volunteered to work in the hospital stores while Zosia still recovered from the effects of her mysterious fever.

Liberation

(Bergen-Belsen, 15 April 1945)

You came – angels on roaring tanks.
Faces blackened by the fires of battle,
uniforms tattered,
hearts – kind.

Sergeant, remember the sunny day in April,
main road between the barracks,
crowds of people shouting, crying?
You shared with me your ration – an egg, a jar of jam.
I didn't stretch my hands towards your gifts.
I felt like one who, facing God, forgets her needs.

Your face looked blurred, my throat gripped
with life's pain, death's pain.
Like Lazarus blinded
Regret wept an ancient song,
sorrowful music echoed
in every cell of my body.

Before you came our guards,
like dogs sensing their master,
relaxed their grip.
Their faces looked human, afraid.
On their arm a symbol of surrender:
a snow-white band.

On clear nights,
though the moon was bright,
we heard rumbling thunder:
flashes of explosion
tore starlit skies.
Afraid to sleep
we stared into darkness
lit with hope.

When you came,
prisoners in the men's camp
tore down the wire fence
and in a wild rush ran to freedom.
The half-dead died.
Their unburied corpses
stretched out their limbs
as though in hope
that through a decent burial
you'd liberate their souls.
Thus we were freed.

How lucky
to die so many deaths
and to stay alive.

The British soldiers who liberated us deserved to be called angels.
They were truly brothers, eager to take care of their skeletal sisters.
They brought us extra bits of furnishings to make our new home more
comfortable. They even managed to find an old-fashioned gramophone and some records – unfortunately, only with German songs.
'Haben Sie einmal in Dunkeln gekusst?' stuck in my memory, maybe
because of the words: 'Have you ever kissed in the dark?'
    We went for our meals to a cafeteria set up by distinguished lady

volunteers from England. I'll never forget a feeling of surprise and gladness when I noticed that one of them had a carefully mended tear in her silk shirt. At once I felt a common bond with them – they'd also experienced deprivations and shortages during those long war years, and they must have suffered greatly during the air raids. At that time I wasn't aware how terribly and interminably London had been bombed during those years.

These ladies served us our meals. Daily I was tormented by misgivings and embarrassment – no matter how much I ate, I had to line up again and again, as if my stomach had become a bottomless container; it never seemed to be full, and my hunger was never appeased. I blushed and apologized and lined up for one more serving. Our helpers didn't mind – they invited us to return as many times as we wished. So we ate, and gradually our bodies became less skeletal, our faces less drawn.

One day three of our liberators – Darkie, John, and George – came with great, joyous news. They'd managed to borrow a car for the following Sunday from a Polish captain, Dr Zietek, who served in their unit as a medical officer – and they were going to take us for a picnic in the woods. We were overjoyed, as we so well remembered that beautiful, ancient forest that we saw after disembarking from the cattle train. 'Nothing bad can happen to us in this beautiful forest,' we had mused, naively and hopefully.

On Sunday the soldiers appeared, soon after lunch, with their car and with picnic food in a basket – lots of spam in the sandwiches, some cookies, and refreshing fruit drinks. The drive along the road in the forest was breathtaking. Last time we had been here had been on a day in March, with snowflakes falling into our faces and onto the dark branches of the evergreens. Now, it was a glorious day in May. Wild flowers covered the forest floor. John turned into a side road and stopped by a lovely meadow. Clusters of buttercups next to meadow sweets, white daisies, and Queen Anne's lace delighted our senses.

We enjoyed the food and attempted to talk to our friends. I was trying to resurrect, from under the heavy blanket of forgetting, my high school English. I said something, and no one seemed to understand. John spoke with a Scottish accent, and young Darkie spoke a bit more clearly, but George was an enigma – maybe he was Welsh. So we gave up and busied ourselves with picking the wild flowers.

But the guys wanted to communicate more, this time through a dance and a song. They danced a dance that was not familiar to any of us. Even Klara Jastroch, my English teacher in Warsaw, missed this one. We found this 'Hokey-Pokey' song and dance quite hilarious:

'You put your right hand in,
you put your right hand out,
You do a Hokey-Pokey
and you turn yourself about.'

They went through the whole routine to our great delight. We laughed and applauded, and we couldn't believe our eyes: these funny, unsophisticated, warm-hearted young men had been just days earlier willing to give their lives in this terrible war, and now they wanted to teach us how to dance the 'Hokey-Pokey' in the middle of this ancient forest, in early May, somewhere in cruel Germany.

We joined in, and now we also felt, for the first time in two years, like young and carefree girls, enjoying this unbelievable outing. Of course, we were young: Zosia was not quite sixteen, I was almost twenty, and Marina was twenty-two. And maybe in this enchanted forest we finally regained our joy of life, our zest for life, and a sense of entitlement to play again, and the catalysts in this transformation were our young British liberators, towards whom we felt deep, sisterly affection.

15
Concert for Survivors

At the beginning of July there was an announcement that a concert was to be given for the survivors by a violinist named Yehudi Menuhin. Benjamin Britten was to accompany him on the piano. These two names meant nothing to me – I had come out of six years of the dark ages: no concerts, no radios, no newspapers to tell us what went on or 'who was who' in that world outside. But I was thrilled at the prospect of hearing live, classical music. And, above all, the fact that a couple of musicians from England wanted to play for us meant that our need for more than bread was appreciated, that despite our captors' cruel attempts to dehumanize us, we were still recognized and accepted by the world as part of the human race.

Years later, in Canada, I bought a book by Yehudi Menuhin, his autobiography entitled *Unfinished Journey.* I read it with fascination. Finally, I came to page 178, where he writes:

The war in Europe had been over some weeks, the war against Japan had still some weeks to run, when, in July 1945, I returned to Germany, for the first time since the Weimar Republic fell to Hitler. Not this time to the orchestral circuit of my youth, but to play for displaced people, survivors of death camps, where, having nowhere to go, they were still living. Like many in those days, Jew or gentile, I had to impress upon my mind an actuality beyond imagination and to offer the living victims the sorrow, the repentance, the solidarity of the unharmed. I asked the British authorities if I might visit the camps in their sector. The British gave me the permission to go, Gerald Moore agreed to come with me. Then, about a week before our departure, at a party given by the music publishers Boosey and Hawks, I met Benjamin Britten. Returned to England after spending the war years largely in the United States, he too was casting for some commitment to the human condition whose terrible depths had been so newly revealed, and was immediately enthusiastic about my initiative. He urged me to take him and Gerald Moore very gracefully gave way.

Before leaving London, Ben and I made an attempt at rehearsing a repertoire, only, after five minutes, to abandon it: there was so much more than we could ever do, our understanding of each other's approach seemed intuitively sure; we put our trust in luck and musical compatibility, and set off for Germany. We took with us more or less the whole standard violin literature – concerti, sonatas, little pieces – and played it, without rehearsal, two or three times a day, for ten days in the saddest ruins of the Third Reich. In Belsen we played twice in one afternoon. I shall not forget that afternoon as long as I live. The inmates of the camp had been liberated for some weeks earlier, the prison huts burned down, and the ex-prisoners transferred to the adjoining SS barracks, which had, among other comforts, a theater. Men and women alike, our audience was dressed in army blankets fashioned by clever tailors among them into skirts and suits. No doubt the few weeks since their rescue had put a little flesh on their bodies, but to our unaccustomed eyes they seemed desperately haggard, and many were still in hospital.*

I went to the concert and listened, enchanted.

To Yehudi Menuhin

> Trim battle dress
> youthful silhouette
> in your hand – a violin
> Young Orfeo – Yehudi
>
> Slim hand
> guides the bow
> Your audience – human shreds
> fashioning Red Cross handouts
> What an ambiance
> Yesterday's hell

---

*Yehudi Menuhin, *Unfinished Journey* (London: Macdonald and Jane's, 1976), 178.

transformed
into a concert hall

Your heart
harbours no doubts
about your role
in this act of redemption
Nourishment of your music
flows through me
fills me
nurtures me
provides simple strength
and everyday courage
as I re-enter the realm of the living
It follows me forty years later
as I write this homage

Trim battle dress
youthful silhouette
in your hand – a violin
Young Orfeo – Yehudi

I wrote this poem in 1985. Today, as I write these words, it is 12 February 2000. Almost a year ago, on Monday, 8 March, I was in a video shop and I noticed a documentary video on Yehudi Menuhin. Something moved me to rent it, and as I watched it that evening I was touched again by his extraordinary life. The next day, when my daughter, Monika, and my granddaughter, Melanie, came to have dinner with me, I told them how moved I had been seeing these episodes from his life and how it brought back the memories of my encounters with him. That night, in the news, I learned that he was in a hospital in Berlin, recovering from a heart attack. On 12 March a sad announcement in the morning news: 'Early this morning, Yehudi Menuhin died of heart failure. He was 82. On Tuesday he cancelled a concert in Berlin. He died in a Berlin hospital.'

Some years earlier, in Toronto, the spring that the Roy Thomson Hall was opened, I planned to go to my first concert there. The soloist was to be Yehudi Menuhin. Days before the concert I found out where he was staying and I wrote him a letter, introducing myself as one of the survivors present at that memorable concert in Belsen. I expressed my profound gratitude and thanks for his gesture that welcomed me to the world of the living. Next, I went to a florist and selected a beautiful bouquet of flowers: masses of white lilacs, tulips, and daffodils. They were to be delivered the night of the concert to his hotel room. That night as I watched him play and listened to his music, I relived again that unforgettable experience of so many years ago.

A few days later I received a charming note from him:

Feb. 3, 1983

Dear Lilka Croydon,

I cannot possibly express my emotion to you as I read your touching letter attached to the glorious flowers.

It meant more than I can say.

The memory of that faraway event as recalled by you moved me deeply. All my warmest thoughts (you did not come backstage. Perhaps next time)

In gratitude,

Yehudi Menuhin

Next time was two years later. I sent him flowers again and attached two of my poems: 'Liberation, Bergen-Belsen' and 'To Yehudi Menuhin.' This time, after the concert, I went backstage. There was a short line-up in his dressing room. When my turn came to talk to him I introduced myself. I don't recall what he said, but I do remember his warm hug. I also recall being a bit surprised that he was much shorter than I remembered, but then, maybe our heroes will always be much larger in our fantasy than in reality.

When the news of his death came, the CBC radio program *Classics and Beyond* devoted the entire morning to his memory, and host Shelagh Rogers inserted, between his compositions, interesting events from his long life. However, she didn't mention his generous humanitarian gesture when he and Benjamin Britten played for ten days to the shreds of humanity in the liberated concentration camps in Germany, in July 1945. At the end of the program I phoned the CBC and left a message, thanking Shelagh Rogers for the beautiful homage to him and also reminding her of this important act. On Monday, as she continued her tribute to Menuhin, she announced that after the eleven

o'clock news there would be a very moving message from an anony-
mous listener relating to his life. True enough, my recorded message
went on the air, followed by more music by my hero.

It's interesting that even though I went to a number of concerts
given by Yehudi Menuhin while I lived in London, England, and later
in Toronto, it took me so long to feel entitled to make my gesture of
gratitude. To feel gratitude towards a great man is one thing – to
express it to him, another. It requires a greater sense of self-confidence
and of entitlement, and this took a while to develop.

After some time the first group of soldiers that liberated us was transferred, and new soldiers appeared. But now the situation was somewhat different: these fellows didn't see us with rags over our skeletal
bodies, and they couldn't feel the same deep, brotherly compassion
towards us. They saw us as young and maybe even quite attractive
females. So it was up to us to create an appropriate distance and establish new ways of relating.

I had no romantic interest in any of them, as now I believed that I
was closer than ever to finding Jerzy. Marina must have been going
through a delayed mourning for her beloved Janek. After we were liberated, we told her the terrible truth about his death. She wasn't surprised. She said that as no one ever mentioned his name she'd figured
out the reason for this avoidance. And Zosia? She enjoyed the company of young Darkie and seemed eager to practise her English with
him. But now he was gone, and we were making new friends.

One was a young Scot named Mac, who had a wife in Newcastle. He
was kind and gentle and invited me one day for a drive. I did go, but
after a while the car stopped and he was not able to get it started. I
didn't know anything about cars, but I was learning something about
Mac as his arm wrapped around my shoulder. I thanked God for my
high school English. I gently removed his arm and had a serious talk
with him: 'Mac, you and I are friends, just friends, OK?' He was sweet
and said 'OK.' The car miraculously started up, and after a lovely drive
through the beautiful forest we headed back to my quarters.

Then there was a young student of theology. We went for walks and
tried to carry on interesting conversations. That meant that he talked
and I mostly listened. I knew that he liked me, but he was gentle and
reserved, and I was happy about this friendship. I talked to him about
Jerzy and my hope that we would soon meet. After I told him that my

proper name wasn't Lilka but Helena, he wrote a poem for me, 'To Fair Helena.' Unfortunately, this poem got lost during the many moves and changes that followed. I'd love to have it now so that I could quote its gentle sentiment.

The communication network that developed within the International Red Cross during the weeks following the liberation of the German camps must have been very extensive. Thanks to it we managed to locate our brother in Buchenwald. To my great joy we found out that it might be possible for us to obtain transportation to visit Tytus. Zosia and I decided to take this opportunity. We were assigned a young British scout, who was to drive us in his jeep to Buchenwald and then bring us back.

We packed a few necessities and met the young driver, who may have been about nineteen. He seemed either terribly shy or simply scared of us. I made several attempts at conversation but without much success.

We admired the beautiful countryside on the way to Buchenwald, which was in the American Zone of occupation. I don't recall how many hours it took us to get there, or how many stops we made on the way. My mind must have been full of anticipation, as well as of hope that Tytus might know Jerzy's whereabouts. So far, all my efforts to locate him had failed.

After the first greetings and hugs, Tytus, disregarding the fact that Zosia was now much taller than he was, took her on his knee and proceeded to comment, with delight, on her beautiful teeth. Before our arrest they were quite crooked – now they were straight!

Unfortunately, Tytus couldn't give me any information about Jerzy. By the time his transport had arrived in Buchenwald Jerzy was not there any longer. He must have been moved to one of the many satellite work camps in the area. Tytus had also lost contact with Father, who was moved to another satellite camp.

In discussing our plans for the near future, we all agreed that we would not return to Poland at this time. The unjust and tragic agreement made by Churchill, Roosevelt, and Stalin at Yalta placed Poland, after six cruel years of German domination, under Communist rule. There were rumours – later proved only too true – that the Communists were executing the remaining members of the Home Army or sending them to Siberia. Tytus told us about one of his friends who decided to go back home – a few days after his departure, a letter arrived from his mother begging him not to return. But the letter came too late.

We stayed overnight in Buchenwald, and the following morning our young driver took us back to Bergen-Belsen. When we arrived there, Marina was waiting impatiently for the news. We told her about our visit and that Tytus might come to visit us soon.

16
Capriccio Italiano

In the meantime we inquired about how to continue our education away from Poland. Our identity as students was very strong. Our studies had been interrupted by our arrest, and my sisters and I were determined to be back at school by September. We had missed two years already, while our friends, if they weren't killed in the Warsaw Uprising, moved ahead of us in their studies.

We contemplated various possibilities. Marina could go to Brussels to continue architectural studies, as she had some French. One day a delegation arrived from Norway. That country was offering educational opportunities to younger students, and Zosia considered this option. But the most tempting prospect was in Italy. General Anders, commander of the Polish Second Corps, part of the Allied forces occupying Italy, was opening two high schools there for young male and female Polish refugees from Germany. There were also prospects of studies at Italian universities. Finally, the three of us agreed that studies in Italy would fulfil all our needs and more. Italy, we knew from our classical studies, was the home of great cultural treasures in art and architecture. The prospect of living in a Mediterranean climate was also incredibly seductive after two dark years of imprisonment.

We discovered that to realize this dream we needed transportation to Meppen, where the Polish General Maczek had his headquarters. His army had fought together with the British and now was occupying Germany – in the British Zone. We learned that the last official transport had left for Italy a couple of days before, but a small military truck was leaving for Italy in a couple of days. The officer in charge had been sent to Germany to search for family members of other officers stationed in Italy – he had not found all the relatives, and so there would be space for the three of us.

In Meppen we registered as members of the Home Army. This was facilitated by Mrs Czarnocka, one of the officers who was with us in Auschwitz and knew the circumstances of our arrest. With great joy we shed our Red Cross handouts and dressed in khaki army shirts and skirts. We offered the Red Cross fashions to a friend from Warsaw, Danka Zdanowicz, who, together with her fiancé, Jan Rossman, was returning to Poland to get married.

In Meppen we also found Tytus. He had also chosen Italy, but for the time being he was running a little school for Polish children while their parents arranged for immigration to the countries that were accepting Polish refugees. Tytus was asked to sign an official affidavit permitting the three of us to travel to Italy to join General Anders's high school.

On 17 September 1939, the Red Army had invaded Poland. It defeated the Polish army, which under the command of General Anders was defending the eastern borders, and deported it to the Soviet Union, along with huge numbers of civilians, especially the intelligentsia – a total of one million people. When Germany and the Soviet Union declared war against each other in 1941, General Anders remobilized and proceeded towards the Middle East, to Palestine, to join the Allies on the North African front.

After the Allied invasion and defeat of Italy, General Anders's Second Corps occupied Italy, together with the British and American armies. In the Second Corps there were many members of the Polish intelligentsia, and from this pool General Anders drew the staff of teachers who were qualified to teach in the two schools.

We left Meppen and were on our way south. Our plan was to travel through the Alps and through the Brenner Pass to Italy. It must have been a breathtakingly beautiful trip, but I remember only two aspects of it. First, Zosia suffered from motion sickness; during a stop in the Alps, she climbed the side of a mountain and declared that she wouldn't go any further in the truck. Of course, after a while, she climbed down, and we continued on our way. Second, we stopped to spend a night at a German guest house. The Polish officer in charge of this trip ordered the owner to prepare the rooms to accommodate us in comfort. I realized that roles had been reversed: Germans now took orders from Poles.

We drove past Innsbruck and through the Brenner Pass to the Italian Alps. From here on, all the signs were in Italian, and my heart rejoiced at the thought of being in Italy. Soon we saw vineyards and peach orchards – the driver, once in a while, stopped the car and ran out to gather handfuls of peaches for us to taste. They were warm from the sun and, oh, so sweet, so delicious. The driver varied his gifts with clusters of grapes, also ripening in the vineyards.

We stopped in Macerata at the headquarters of the commandant of the Women's Auxiliary Services, Captain Wyslouchowa. The officer in charge introduced the three of us as candidates for studies in Italy. We identified ourselves as members of the Home Army and presented our affidavits from Meppen. We were informed that the high school for girls would be located in Porto San Giorgio, a small seaside town on the Adriatic coast. However, as final preparations for our accommodation there were not complete, we would spend several days in a transit camp in Macerata.

As we had arrived rather late in the day, Captain Wyslouchowa offered to put us up for the night in her villa. Next day we were transported to the local camp in Macerata.

Marina was sent to work in a cartographic company until university studies started and Zosia and I left for Porto San Giorgio.

The beauty of Italy was overwhelming. The vineyards, the olive groves, the fields covered with sunflowers in full bloom, the cypress trees, the small hill towns – we felt that we had entered another world. Under the blue skies and in the warmth of the Italian sun we would replenish our energies and heal our bruised souls.

Porto San Giorgio was located south of Ancona, in the Marche district. It was a small fishing village at the foot of a splendid castle that the Bonapartes had owned but was now to serve as our residence. Impressive wide stairs led to a portico with great columns gracing the entrance. My dormitory had windows looking out on the little village, on the beach with the fishing boats, and on the resplendent Adriatic. Other windows overlooked scattered farms with vineyards and the ever-present olive groves.

We met our house-mother, Mrs Tomaszewska, whose daughter Hanka was in Zosia's class. I also met my five room-mates. Soon I developed a friendship with Zosia Gorska. She was very friendly and cheerful and we spent many hours studying together. She wrote poetry, and under her influence I started to write too. I have kept one of my poems from those days, but I have never translated it into English. It is a nostalgic piece about Warsaw and my sad goodbye to it, at dawn, on 13 May 1943.

While we waited for our classes to begin, we enjoyed the beach to the full – the splendour of the warm Adriatic and the white, sandy shore. This was my first experience of swimming in the sea, and I was somewhat timid about venturing too far from shore. But I asked the friendly fishermen to take me far out to sea in their boats. Then I would swim back to the beach.

In no time my body, not used to the strong sun, turned very red, and before I noticed I had a severe sunburn. Somebody suggested sour cream for soothing the burn, and my room-mates smeared it all over my back and shoulders. True enough, I was back on the beach within days – this time more careful about too much sun.

Our school building was located in Porto San Giorgio. It must have been the public school for the local children – I never found out where they studied that year. All our teachers were women from the Second Corps, liberated from the Soviet gulags.

Zosia Gorska and I loved getting up at sunrise. The countryside was fresh and cool as the two of us would set out, with our books, on a hike around the vineyards. We quizzed each other in history or Latin, and when we had had enough of Latin we sang, at the top of our lungs, a variety of Polish songs, while the farmers started their daily chores.

Our group of girls included insurgents from the Warsaw Uprising; there were also others who had survived the Soviet gulags. Despite our turbulent pasts, we were all young and not devoid of mischief. I recall our night-time adventures at the seashore. After the lights were out, we were supposed to stay in our dormitories. However, the nights were so beautiful and warm that sometimes, after our house-mother was asleep, we would sneak out and run down through the sleepy little town to the beach for a skinny-dip. The fireflies were like silver rain all around us, and the stars above were reflected in the water, melting in the warm waves of the Adriatic. These excursions were never discovered – or, if they were, no one ever reprimanded us for them.

Our curriculum – for the final year of high school – had all the regular subjects, including English and Latin, but I missed Italian. In Italy, we should have been studying Italian. So I made inquiries in town, and soon a teacher was giving me private lessons. As a soldier in the Second Corps I received a monthly ration of cigarettes. I didn't smoke, and I used my cigarettes to pay my Italian teacher for the lessons. This went on for some time, but in the new year she announced that we would have to discontinue because she was leaving for Rome. I was dismayed. I didn't look for another teacher, though – the school work was piling up, and I wanted to have the best possible results on my diploma. I even sacrificed a trip to Venice one weekend before a couple of exams. I regretted that decision for years – until I visited Italy again, many times, from Canada.

Sometime during that glorious year I developed horrid carbuncles all over my body. High fever accompanied these painful sores, and it was determined that I should spend some time in a military hospital in Ancona. I felt that Auschwitz was pouring out of me through those carbuncles. In hospital, with medication, my condition improved gradually, and I returned to my dorm in the castello.

On Palm Sunday weekend our school organized a trip to Gubbio. We arrived on Saturday morning and explored that charming town. On Sunday I awoke to the sound of bells. It seemed that the whole town was swinging and ringing as each of its many churches put on a magnificent concert. These unforgettable sounds carried me back to Warsaw, where the bells of the Church of the Redeemer, just a couple of blocks from our home, sounded loud and clear every Sunday morning. But never again have I heard so many bells ringing as that morning in Gubbio. We celebrated mass in one of the churches and, after lunch, returned to Porto San Giorgio, with the great bells of Gubbio still ringing in my ears, still flowing in my blood.

> Glad years, embrace me,
> let me rest in the hospitable shade
> of ancient olive trees.
> Europe's dark winter gone.
> Demeter's wistful smile once more
> grants Spring to blood-washed earth.
>
> Radiant days!
> Let me wander, wrapped in warm sunshine,
> through thyme-scented vineyards,

let me sing alleluias
in gold and blue syllables of Florentine angels.
Let me inhabit Giotto's wondrous frescos.
Infuse me with Leonardo's strong softness,
adorn me in ephemeral garments
of Botticelli's Spring.
Warm fields of Tuscany
take me back.
Gentle waves of the Adriatic
soothe my pain-touched body.
Mediterranean grottoes
fill my horror-visited eyes
with your azure splendour.

Take me back
soft sienna of Assisi churches,
Palm Sunday bells of Gubbio,
warm nights on the sea
where fireflies' elusive brilliance
competed with the stars
and stars – liquid jewels
skipped on jet-black waves.

We were not allowed to fraternize with the Italian male population. Our social life was limited to an occasional weekend dance at a neighbourhood Polish army unit. A military truck would arrive and take us to the dance. I can't say that we enjoyed these excursions – we had so little in common with those fellows. But it was fun to remember the steps of tangos or foxtrots or waltzes. Once, my dancing partner became very enthusiastic about me and suggested that after I received my high school diploma he would like to take me to 'America,' where we would marry and live happily ever after. He was a simple fellow and could not comprehend that I might have different plans. I thanked him for his kind offer.

There was no news from Poland, and there was no word about Father or Jerzy. Fortunately I was so busy and so enchanted with Italy that this uncertainty was not weighing too heavily on me. As Warsaw was totally destroyed during and after the uprising, it was obvious that it would be very difficult to locate anyone – the civilian population had been driven out of the city and the remaining buildings dynamited. Later on I found out that Jerzy's father and mother and his sister Irena had moved to Gdansk, on the Baltic Sea, where Jerzy's father carried on with his medical practice while Warsaw was being slowly rebuilt.

My final exams were close, and I devoted myself wholly to my studies. The school was not organizing any more trips so I didn't feel that I was missing much. When the time came for the examinations, I felt confident and well prepared. My final results were excellent, and I was happy that I didn't disappoint myself and my teachers. I still have my diploma in a drawer, my young face on the photograph looking into the unknown future.

When the school year ended I set out for Rome. Zosia Gorska headed for Paris to study at the Sorbonne. She had received a scholarship from the Catholic Church. Halszka Forbert, whose father was an officer in the Second Corps, immigrated with him to Sweden. Other classmates went in many directions, depending on their interests and opportunities.

It was a lovely sunny day, at the end of June 1946. I was almost twenty-one, with my high school diploma in my bag, and at that moment it seemed to me that the world was at my feet. I was looking forward to visiting Rome, the city of my dreams, of which I had read so much. The thought of visiting the Colosseum, where, in Henryk Sienkiewicz's *Quo Vadis*, the Romans threw beautiful Lydia to the lions, filled me with great anticipation. I would visit the Vatican with its magnificent St Peter's Basilica and its museums. I had also heard about great opera performances during summer months in the Termae di Caracalla, under the cupola of the starry sky. The thought of living for the next two months in this ancient city filled me with joy and excitement. Of course, I would be working, and at this point I had no idea what my job would be. But I knew that there would be weekends and long summer evenings when I could explore every nook and cranny of that holy city.

Despite my anticipation, I was sad to leave Porto San Giorgio. There, by the shores of the beautiful Adriatic, I had returned to life. There I was able to complete high school as well as to take in the beauty of Italy. When would I come back to this sleepy little town that had offered me so much?

I did return forty years later, in 1985. It was summer again, and as I descended from the train and walked through the town I was struck by the changes. From a quiet little fishing village, Porto San Giorgio had turned into a charming resort town, a favourite vacation place of the Romans, who were staying in fashionable new hotels and shopping in elegant boutiques.

I registered in one of the hotels, with windows overlooking my favourite sea. I was not the only guest there from North America – a basketball team from California, a team of tall African Americans, was going to play against the Italians. On the beach they towered like Gullivers over everyone else and were a true sensation of the town.

After dinner I observed that all the guests set out for a walk along the wide boardwalk, which was new to me. I decided to do as the Romans did and set out for a walk every night, after dinner. A few days later, as I was walking alone, I was suddenly surrounded by a group of young Italians, both male and female. There was even a small bambino, Matteo, pushed in his carriage by his proud young mama.

One of the young men asked what I was doing in Porto San Giorgio. I replied that I belonged to the history of the little town. They wished to know what I meant by that. So I proceeded to explain that forty years earlier I had lived there as a young student. My residence was in the castello, my school was in town. They showed great surprise. I suggested that they talk to their parents and their grandparents. They would remember the occupation of Italy, after the liberation, by the Allies. They might remember the Polish army of General Anders. They might even remember the Polish girls who lived in the castello. After some discussion, one of the young men suggested that we meet the next day, at eleven, by the castello. I agreed, with pleasure. As I walked back to my hotel, I mused about this interesting encounter – these young local people must have observed, with curiosity, this middle-aged woman, emancipated and autonomous, wandering through their town, obviously feeling at home here. Why was she here?

The next day, as I was climbing the path towards the castello, I saw my young friends gathered by the wide front steps. Little Matteo was there, as well. I joined them and pointed to the windows of my old dorm. At that time an old gardener appeared. He looked oddly familiar, and to my surprise it turned out that he had been at the castello all these years, looking after the grounds. Yes, he remembered the Polish signorinas, yes, forty years ago. One of the young men suggested that he take a photograph of me, sitting on the wide steps leading to the entrance. We said 'ciao' to the gardener and walked together to the beach.

Before we parted, someone suggested that we meet on Saturday for the basketball match. I was sorry that I had to say no, but I was leaving on that day for Sienna.

There was no direct train from Porto San Giorgio to Rome, so I took a train to Ancona, where I waited for the train to Rome. My train finally arrived, and after finding my compartment, I settled down in my seat. My compartment was not crowded. There were some civilians and a number of military men.

Across from me sat a Polish Second Corps officer. The sleeves of my army shirt were rolled up. He was staring at the Auschwitz tattoo on my left arm. Finally, apologizing, he explained: 'My wife, Lusia Kiel-anowska, had a number close to yours. Did you by any chance know her in Birkenau? Do you remember her?' I knew that Lusia's husband was a theatre director in Wilno, but I had no idea that he would be here, in the Polish Second Corps. To his question I replied that yes, I knew her, and that I would never forget her. I proceeded to tell him about our work in the herb *Kommando* and about her wonderful way of entertaining us at lunch breaks, when she recited parts from various plays. I told him how warm and friendly she was and how everyone loved her. I also described to him the incident with the cherry tree and my gratitude to her for making us aware of the importance of preserving our dignity even when we felt extremely hungry and needy.

Tears were streaming down our faces as our train approached the ancient walls of Rome. At the station we parted, knowing that this meeting would remain in our memory for a long time. A taxi carried me to the area of Rome where the Church of Santa Maria Maggiore towered over other buildings. My new quarters were located in the Women's Auxiliary Services Hostel, close to this church.

Epilogue

While still in Rome I learned that Father was alive and well in a displaced persons' camp in Germany.

After our arrest my grandmother moved in with one of her other sons. Aunt Lucia moved to Krakow after our arrest and lived there with her brother, Lucjan, and his family.

All efforts to find Jerzy failed. His parents, in Poland, used all possible means, but they could learn only that he was registered in Buchenwald camp files as alive, working at a satellite camp called Taucha, right up until the liberation of the camp.

Later on some rumours came that someone saw him in Leipzig, waiting for a repatriation train to Poland. Those trains also carried Soviet prisoners, returning from prisoner-of-war camps in Germany. As the Soviet authorities considered these prisoners traitors because they were captured alive and also corrupted by the fascists who held them captive, the trains carrying them would pass Poland, stop somewhere in the middle of Siberia, and all the passengers would be executed. Was this also Jerzy's fate?

The Medics Club

Joanna Berland survived the 1944 Warsaw Uprising, studied to become an oncologist, and married Wojtek Makolski. Their daughter, Hanka, lives in Philadelphia, is married, and has one daughter. However, Joanna divorced Wojtek and later married Mieczyslaw Kowalski, a man thirty years older than she. He was a general and also a physician. He died at the age of ninety-three.

Marysia Wysowska also studied medicine and became a laryngologist.

Wanda Jedraszko became a dentist and immigrated to Paris.

After some years as a special education teacher, I retrained to become a child and adolescent psychoanalyst and continue to work in private practice. I've lived in Toronto since November 1948. I was married for twenty-five years to Peter Croydon. I left him in 1973. I have two children: Monika, born in 1952, and Janek, born in 1956. Janek immigrated to New Zealand in 1988 and lives in Auckland with his wife, Ellen, and their three children. Monika, after eight years of marriage to David Sugarman, was divorced. They have one daughter, Melanie, born in 1988. They live in Toronto.

The Fate of Others

My father died in Toronto, in 1963, of heart failure, after shovelling snow on his sidewalk. He was sixty-eight. He'd lived in Toronto since 1949.

My sister Marina became an architect in London, England. She and her husband Marek Pain, also an architect, came to Toronto in 1951. In 1952 she gave birth to her daughter, Magda. Marina died of cancer in 1975. Her daughter lives in Toronto with her husband, John Smith, and their two teenagers, Alexander and Cathrine.

My brother Tytus, after finishing his studies in engineering, came from England to Chicago, where he still lives. He married a Chilean woman, Amalia, and has three children and six grandchildren. Amalia died in 2001.

My sister Zosia became a nurse. She married George Jeffs. There are two children, Jennifer and Greg, both married. Jennifer has three children, and she and her family currently live in Mexico City. George Jeffs died in 1988. Zosia moved to Ottawa in 1993 and to Barry's Bay, Ontario, in 2002. She died of cancer in the spring of 2004.

'Our bed of love is made among the lions' dens'
                          – St John of the Cross

Kampinos Forest
heather meadow
cricket's song
cobalt-blue skies of autumn

Our world pervaded by fear
the enemy waited in the streets
lightless nights full of phantoms
the murderers' song entering our dreams
its sharp edge slashing our hopes

We escaped into this forest
that held secrets of buried guns
we escaped into the shade of ancient trees
we escaped with our newborn love
and held it firmly in our hearts

Your face your hands
a quickened heartbeat
in my sixteen-year-old breast
enclosed in a love circle forever
for love like eternity is one

We've guarded it through those years
by the banks of the Acheron
through war and fear and hunger

I brought it to the other shore of an ocean
where I've pitied the sun the moon the stars
that shone on the world without you
and I mourned the tiny buds of heather
since then turned into ash

I unpetal stars for you
they know your mystery
where and when it was
and under what skies

you felt your last heartbeat
as you whispered
I love you I love you I love you
these words breathed life into me

Soon we shall wander together
among the stars that glow in the sky
like those tiny white daisies
on the meadows in our country

Years tumble around me
all the Nativities and all the Resurrections
always you always our love
always the heather meadow
always the cobalt-blue skies of autumn

15 December 1996.
For Jerzy's 75th Birthday.

Illustration Credits

Danuta Bytnar-Dziekanska: Marina Trzcinska and Janek 'Rudy' Bytnar, spring 1942.

Lilka Croydon: Felicja Masiukiewicz, 1912; Zosia, Lilka, Marina, and Tytus, 1931; three Trzcinska sisters, 1935; grandfather's funeral, 1936; Lilka Trzcinska in Porto San Giorgio, 1945; General Anders's Girls' School in Porto San Giorgio, 1945; view from Lilka's dormitory, 1945; Easter 1946 – lunch in Porto San Giorgio; Zosia Trzcinska, Porto San Giorgio, 1946; students from Lilka Trzcinska's class, 1946; arms with Auschwitz tattoos, 1946; Zosia and Lilka Trzcinska, Porto San Giorgio, 1946; Lilka Trzcinska in Porto San Giorgio, 1946; Marina Trzcinska and Alicja Sieciechowicz in Porto Recanati, 1946; Tytus Trzcinski, in General Anders's army, 1946; Zosia Gorska, Porto San Giorgio, 1946.

Wojtek Makolski: Josef Pleszczynski; Jedrek Makolski; Wojtek Makolski, Warsaw, 1946.

Dr Irena Masiukiewicz-Groszkowska: Jerzy Masiukiewicz, Jacek Tabecki, and Alek Dawidowski, on a skiing trip; Jerzy's name-day celebration; Lilka Trzcinska, 1942; Lilka Trzcinska and Jerzy Masiukiewicz, spring 1942; Marina Trzcinska, Irena Masiukiewicz, Joanna Berland, and Lilka Trzcinska on the banks of the Vistula River, summer 1942; Janek Bytnar, Warsaw, 1942; Jerzy Masiukiewicz; Marina Trzcinska, Wladek Slodkowski, Lilka Trzcinska, and Jerzy Masiukiewicz, 1942, by the banks of the Vistula River; Irena Masiukiewicz, Marina Trzcinska, and Joanna Berland by the banks of the Vistula River, 1942; Jacek Tabecki, Andrzej Zawadowski, and Tytus Trzcinski, Warsaw, 1942;

Tytus Trzcinski, Danuta Bytnar, Lilka Trzcinska, Janek Bytnar, Tadeusz Kozlowski, and Marina Trzcinska on the road to Kampinos Forest; Tadeusz Kozlowski, Wladek Slodkowski, Marina Trzcinska, Janek Bytnar, Jerzy Masiukiewicz, and Lilka Trzcinska; Andrzej Zawadowski.